# FOOD FOR THOUGHT

Fr NEIL McNICHOLAS

# FOOD FOR THOUGHT

## Sunday sermons that might have been – but for the homily

ST PAULS

ST PAULS Publishing
187 Battersea Bridge Road, London SW11 3AS, UK
www.stpaulspublishing.com



ISBN 978-0-85439-809-6

A catalogue record is available for this book from the British Library.

Set by Tukan DTP, Stubbington, Fareham, UK
Printed by Intype Libra Ltd, Wimbledon, London, UK

ST PAULS is an activity of the priests and brothers
of the Society of St Paul who proclaim the Gospel
through the media of social communication.

# CONTENTS

**Introduction** 9

**"Sixpence in the Slot" Priests** 11
In defence of the priest's role and responsibility to teach "in season and out", as Scripture says, when people may prefer not to hear what he has to say because of its implications for them.

**Feeding our Faith, Sustaining our Parish** 14
In the current climate of parishes having to be amalgamated and churches having to close, the degree to which people are involved in their faith community may well determine its future.

**Is Christianity Becoming a Crime?** 19
This article was written in response to "political correctness" and attempts to dumb-down the claim that ours is a Christian country.

**Living Together – Living Apart** 25
An invitation to couples living together to consider putting their situation right as the Church sees it. Also some important pastoral information with regard to the sacraments for people who are separated or divorced.

**A Pilgrim People – "Follow Me"** 30
This article discusses the need to trust in the guidance of the Holy Spirit as the Church moves forward in its journey of faith, as opposed to the rather sad alternative of remaining anchored in the past.

**Halloween** 34
People seem to have become very blasé about some of the activities and symbols attached to Halloween. The intention of this pastoral reflection is to encourage them to be more realistic and more aware.

**Where Are All The People?** 40
An invitation to consider our shared call to the work of evangelisation and the suggestion that if we were carrying out that work as fully as perhaps we should be, then our churches might be a little fuller.

**A Continuum of Pastoral Care** 44

This article presents important information which Catholics should know about in the area of pastoral care of the sick, the dying and the bereaved.

**Clericalism v Accountability** 50

In some respects this article would make good reading for the clergy, but my purpose was to explain to lay people the extent to which priests, as stewards, should be accountable to them.

**Communion Under Both Kinds** 55

A pastoral invitation, especially to those who receive only the host, to consider experiencing the fullness of the sacrament.

**Meatless Fridays** 60

It would seem that when abstaining from meat went by the board we thought we could forget about Fridays. For forty-five years it has been a particularly well-kept secret that that isn't, in fact, the case.

**Aspects of Lent** 65

This article looks at various aspects of the season of Lent and offers some thoughts on better appreciating the meaning of our Lenten practices and symbols.

***The Passage of Time*** 71

The pace of society causes us to be constantly planning ahead to the point that we fail to live in, and savour, the present.

**A Family Divided** 75

This is a reflection on Christian unity, admitting that there continue to be things that, sadly, divide us – issues that are beyond our personal influence other than through our prayers.

**If Only We Had Known Better** 80

This article addresses the sensitive and difficult issue of child abuse by priests.

**On a More Positive Note** 87

This article seeks to provide a more positive picture of priesthood and the ministry of priests than the one currently being painted by the media.

**Honestly?** 93
A reflection on truth and honesty and the potential ill-effects of what can become almost casual lying. Also the issue of trust and keeping confidences.

**Putting Christ Back into Christmas** 98
My annual attempt to try to get people to focus on the true meaning of Christmas and to resist the premature excesses of the High Street.

**Vocations** 104
A few reflections by way of encouraging those whom God may be calling to priesthood or religious life to be open to that possibility. An encouragement, too, for prayer for vocations.

**Faith, Hope and Love** 109
The title speaks for itself.

**God Willing** 114
How much of an effort do we put into trying honestly and prayerfully to determine God's will for us? And what if our prayers are not answered in the way we hoped?

**Forming Our Conscience** 120
We are morally obliged to follow our conscience, but this begs the question as to whether we have fully and properly formed our conscience in the first place.

**"Late Have I Loved You"** 125
Late-coming at Mass: a hobby horse of mine!

**Being Clothed in Christ and for Christ** 131
Some thoughts on our Christian vocation from the time we are clothed with Christ at baptism and a reflection on the appropriateness (or otherwise) of how we dress for church.

**Relics** 136
Following the recent visit to this country of the relics of St Thérèse, some pastoral reflections for those who may have felt a bit guilty because they didn't share the euphoria that accompanied that visit.

**Sacraments: A Constant Source of Grace** 142
A reflection on the help and strength and grace the sacraments provide at various stages throughout our lives, and the unique place of the Eucharist as "the source and summit" of our Christian life.

**The Priesthood of the Baptised** 148
We are constantly reminded that we are a "royal priesthood", but what does this mean in practical terms?

**Envy – An 'Owner's Manual'** 153
Looking at the subject of envy using quotations from various writers as well as my own thoughts on the subject.

**Prayer** 158
Some general thoughts and suggestions on prayer.

**Humus, Humilis** 163
How do we understand humility and what does it mean to be grounded in our faith?

**Being a Part, Not Being Apart** 169
An appeal to active participation in our Eucharistic celebrations, a recurring theme throughout the Bishops' Conference document *Celebrating the Mass*.

**Fit for the Race** 175
How spiritually "fit" are we? How is our spiritual and sacramental life? How involved are we in the spiritual, pastoral and practical life of our parish?

**The Real Presence** 179
What do we believe about the Real Presence of Jesus in the Blessed Sacrament?

**The Power of the Pause** 183
A reflection on the word of God in the Mass and in *lectio divina*.

**Vatican-lite** 189
An invitation to think about our approach to Church teaching.

# INTRODUCTION

When the Second Vatican Council called for priests to give *homilies* based on the Scripture readings of the day rather than the more general traditional Sunday sermon, there were suddenly far fewer opportunities for priests to specifically address areas of spiritual or pastoral need unless the two things happened to coincide – which doesn't seem to happen very often. These pastoral reflections, originally distributed with the parish newsletter, were written in order to do both things at once by providing, on a fairly regular basis, something for people to read in their own time at home, in addition to the homily they had heard at Mass.

In a sense the change of policy introduced by the Council became an example of the poet Robert Frost's "two roads diverging in a wood", and these pastoral reflections have enabled me to take the pastoral road that would otherwise have been less travelled.

Reactions over the years have been mixed with some, at one end of the spectrum, welcoming them enthusiastically, whilst others simply passed them by as they came into church or actually detached them from the newsletter and left them on the table unread. I always find this a bit sad – not because they were ignoring something I had written, but because it was almost as if they hoped to get away with the "where ignorance is bliss" defence when God might one day challenge them on something they really should have known.

Many people have suggested that I should have these reflections published so they could be enjoyed (at least that was the theory!) by a wider audience and that's how this book has now come into being. I hope you enjoy it.

1

# "SIXPENCE IN THE SLOT" PRIESTS

In defence of the priest's role and responsibility to teach "in season and out", as Scripture says, when people may prefer not to hear what he has to say because of its implications for them.

I don't know if amusement arcades still have the "Aladdin's Cave" machines they used to have when I was a youngster. The glass-sided machine was full of "trinkets and treasures" and when you put your sixpence in, an elephant moved round a track into a cave and emerged with a box on its back which then tipped into a chute and inside was your sixpenny prize. Sometimes I think some people expect their priests to be like that. They put their money in the Sunday collection and all they want is for the priest to come out, "say" Mass and disappear again leaving them in peace.

Though it would make for a quiet life, we are not meant to be "sixpence in the slot" priests. Apart from being ministers of the sacraments, priests are also meant to be teachers. Every year at the Chrism Mass we stand before God and our bishop to renew the commitments we made at our ordination and one of the things we are asked is: *Are you resolved to imitate Jesus Christ, the head and shepherd of the Church, by teaching the Christian faith without thinking of your own profit, solely for the well-being of the people you were sent to serve?* People may not always like a particular priest as an individual but they should at least respect his office as priest and teacher. He has been appointed by his bishop acting with the authority handed down from the apostles. Under the guidance of the Holy Spirit he then carries out his ministry as priest and teacher and should never, therefore, misuse or abuse his position, because he is accountable not just to his bishop, but to God.

In this regard I often return to the words of Pope St Gregory the Great:

> A religious leader should be careful in deciding when to remain silent and be sure to say something useful when deciding to speak… Ill-advised silence can leave people in their error, when they could have been shown where they were wrong. Negligent religious leaders are often afraid to speak and say what needs to be said – for fear of losing favour with people.

There used to be a time when "hell and damnation" sermons were commonplace and there were priests who were renowned for them. They may not have made themselves very popular at the time – though I think they were respected just the same – but you couldn't really argue with what they said because by and large they were right. It was just that people didn't like to be reminded of the fact. These days we priests are fairly restricted when it comes to sermons (or 'homilies' as they are now called) because they are supposed to be based on the readings of the day, especially the gospel. As a result, all sorts of other spiritual and pastoral subjects that really need to be addressed tend to go by the board. That is why, a couple of parishes ago, I began writing these attachments to the newsletter which people could read in their own time. Those writings were things I felt needed to be said because the readings of the day did not offer the opportunity. The alternative – to ignore the issue – would be an inexcusable failure and a disservice to the people.

Sadly I have watched parishioners detach these papers from their newsletters and leave them on the table unread presumably because they not only did not want to hear what I had to say, but they do not particularly want to hear *anything* that's being said because it just might have implications for their faith and they'd prefer not to know about it. Similarly it does not seem to matter how many times I mention things like arriving late for Mass, talking in church, taking newsletters home for information… there are some who simply take no notice and these practices continue.

Some of these things may not seem very important in the overall scheme of things, but others certainly are and involve matters of best practice and church teaching. If people feel they can ignore the basic stuff, where does it stop? If we do not get the foundations right, then the structure we build on them is greatly at risk. In some of the older parts of the presbytery there is not a single straight wall – and why? It is because they would appear to have been built at will without any attempt to align them on a cornerstone. Our foundation, our cornerstone, has constantly to be Jesus Christ and the teachings of the Church he founded for our salvation.

One of the concerns that I have as a priest is the possible consequence for those who seem to treat Church teaching like a buffet – picking and choosing according to their personal taste. There is a story you may have heard concerning a man clinging to his rooftop as the rain poured down and the flood waters rose around him. He prays to God to save him but the waters continue to rise. A man in a boat comes by and offers to help him but the man replies that he is a religious man and has every confidence that God will save him. Still the rain pours and the waters rise. A helicopter arrives on the scene but again he refuses their assistance explaining once again that he has every faith in God to save him. The waters continue to rise and eventually the man drowns. When he arrives at the Pearly Gates he asks God how come he did not save him and God replies, 'I sent a man in a row boat and I sent a helicopter, what more did you want?'

One day we will find ourselves standing before God and being asked to give an account of ourselves and our lives. My fear is for those who may be found wanting and who will then try to offer the same excuses they used in life and God will say to them, "But don't you remember Father so-and-so telling you all about that? Don't you remember all those times he explained that to you?" At that point it will be too late to do anything about it. And while other people may only have to give an account to God of themselves, we priests will be accountable for how well (or otherwise) we have served (or failed to serve) the many thousands of people for whom God gave us spiritual and pastoral responsibility throughout our ministry and that's why we can't afford to be "sixpence in the slot" priests.

2

# FEEDING OUR FAITH, SUSTAINING OUR PARISH

> In the current climate of parishes having to be amalgamated and churches having to close, the degree to which people are involved in their faith community may well determine its future.

I have never really liked dates – I'm talking about the fruit. When I was working in Saudi Arabia, my Saudi colleagues just couldn't understand for a moment how anyone could not like something that was so basic to their diet. To them it was automatic that everyone liked dates. Perhaps the same could be said about someone who is passionate about a particular hobby – fishing, train spotting, ballroom dancing, antiques, football – and who may struggle to comprehend how other people can get through life with no such interest whatsoever. In a sense I suppose I feel the same about my faith. Clearly being a priest might be expected to create a heightened involvement in, and commitment to, the practice of my faith, but I'm speaking in a more general sense than that.

It never ceases to amaze me, standing outside church on a Sunday morning, to realise how many people are going about their business with no apparent concept that it's the Lord's Day. I look at all the people strolling past on their way to the paper shop or the supermarket, and few, if any, of them are also on their way to Mass or morning service. I look at the crowds that get themselves out of bed at the crack of dawn in the hope of snapping up a bargain at the local Sunday car boot sale. Would they get up that early for church? Would they get up at all for church? Do they not see salvation as a bargain to be snapped up? For so many people Sunday just doesn't rate and, sadly, neither does God except when they're in trouble and maybe not even then – and that's not me being judgmental, it's simply a fact of modern life. We who believe, and, more specifically, we who practise our faith, are in the minority; there are probably more people at the car boot sale than there will be at church!

How can so many people go through life with no immediate sense of God, much less a declared affiliation to a particular denomination? How can their daily choices and actions be governed by nothing more than their own personal taste or creed? Do we sometimes find ourselves a little envious of such people seemingly freewheeling through life? Is my faith, then, a brake on my freewheeling or is it, rather, something that gives meaning and purpose to my life? Could I imagine my life without my faith? Indeed, could I *deal* with life without my faith?

Church in the sense of going to church has always been important to me. No doubt there was a time when I went to Mass on Sundays because I had to and because if I didn't it was a mortal sin. I well remember one Sunday when my Dad and I set off to Mass (my mother wasn't a Catholic). I was young enough at the time that I could sit on the crossbar of my Dad's bike. I remember him warning me to keep my feet clear of the front wheel and the next thing I knew we were both flying over the handlebars because the front wheel is exactly where one of my feet had gone – we hadn't even left our street yet! I landed first, the bike on top of me, and my Dad on top of the bike and me. He went back home in a huff and I set off, with grazed knees and elbows, to walk the mile to church because I knew I had to go to Mass.

I never went through the typical late-teenage rebellion stage against going to church; there never had to be any of the "As long as you live in this house you'll go to church" stuff from my parents. I just always went. And it seems as if, over the years, I gradually became increasingly involved in the life of my parish and of the Church, eventually pursuing my experience of a vocation to the priesthood. Maybe that's the first question to ask: is our faith only about going to church, as important as that is, or, as we have grown older, has the practice of our faith also matured and found its expression in other areas of involvement?

Statistically, in a typical parish, fewer than 10% of nominal Catholics would be going to Mass on a regular basis and even then not all of them every Sunday despite the fact that it is a mortal sin deliberately not to go without due cause. Nine-out-of-ten nominal Catholics are therefore not even practising their faith at all. Talking with diocesan colleagues and priest-friends elsewhere, typically only about 10% of that Mass-going 10% attend parish meetings, courses and activities (and it's usually the same core group each time) meaning that as many as nine-out-of-ten parishioners are not actively involved in the life of their parish beyond their attendance at Sunday Mass.

I do, of course, appreciate that in any parish a great many people do have other commitments – especially in terms of their work and their family – and are simply not as free as they might like to be in terms of Mass and parish activities. I didn't want you to think that I thought everyone was as free to be involved as priests are (even though some people think we only work on Sundays!). Equally I recognise that many are indeed already involved in various aspects of the life of the parish and so I may be "preaching to the converted" as they say.

"Baptism makes us members of the Body of Christ, therefore we are members one of another. Baptism incorporates us into the Church.[1] The baptised have become living stones to be built into a spiritual house (para. 1268). Having become a member of the Church, the person baptised belongs no longer to him(her)self, but to him who died and rose for us. From now on, he/she is called to be subject to others, to serve them in the communion of the Church (para. 1269). They participate in the apostolic and missionary activity of the People of God." (para. 1270).

What the catechism is saying is that, by virtue of our baptism, we become (in the nicest sense of the words) "split personalities": we belong to the world but we also belong to God, we have a physical self and a spiritual self but the two are indivisible in that we can't just put on our Catholic self on Sundays along with our "Sunday best" clothes. Who we are as people of faith is who we are twenty-four hours a day, seven days a week, fifty-two weeks of the year. Church isn't just somewhere we go or something we do, it's who we are.

Perhaps if the Catholic tradition was to plunge the candidate for baptism into the water of the baptismal pool, we might identify a little more with the symbolism of the fact that we are, or should be, totally immersed in Christ, "dripping with faith" as it were. And it could well be a challenge to many to realise that they are, as the catechism says, "called to serve (others) in the communion of the Church… (and to) participate in the apostolic and missionary activity of the People of God" (para. 1269/70). We can do neither of those properly or well unless we are involved in the life of the Church and of our faith community.

The Church can be likened to a sailing ship, but it's not a cruise ship where we can sit back and relax and let the crew do all the work – we *are* the crew. There are a thousand things that need to be done to keep a sailing ship on course and operating smoothly. If we don't play our part, then the work falls to others who may well be busy enough already. The Holy Spirit is the wind driving the ship forward and anything that we can do to get every ounce out of that wind can only be to our advantage. On the other hand, progress will only be hampered if people keep lowering lifeboats – or the anchor! Enough with the nautical imagery… well, just one more if I may. Unlike with a ship, trying to "press gang" people into service in the Church doesn't work; rather it is hoped that people will volunteer in numbers, out of a passion for, and commitment to, their faith.

I started out with the example of dates and hobbies and the different perception that people can have when they are passionate about something. Yes, I'm going to have a slightly different perspective as a priest and for that reason I try not to set my expectations too high, but it can sometimes be very disappointing when people don't come to things, don't come forward to volunteer their services, don't seem to want to be involved beyond going to Mass. I don't understand it. It's like having a club membership and not being an active member; having a gleaming Rolls and never taking it out of the garage; winning the lottery and burying the winnings in the ground; having a unique talent and never using it.

- Do you manage to get to Mass during the week – could the Eucharist be a more regular part of your week?
- Are there areas of parish life, or ministries, or groups you could be involved in?
- Have you participated in recent courses, programmes or activities offered in the parish?
- If not, was it because they didn't appeal to you?
- What courses, groups or activities *would* appeal – have you suggested them – could you help organise them?

Our parishes will be what we make of them. We are called to do and to give in order to ensure that we also receive; to be active members of worshipping communities that sustain and encourage our faith; to put our God-given talents and abilities at the service of the gospel. Of course, age, health, or personal circumstances may well place unavoidable limitations on what we are able to do and that is understood. We may not be passionate about sports, train spotting, knitting or even dates(!), but we ought to be passionate about our faith – it defines who we are and what we will be and it's a channel for what we do.

NOTE

1 *Catechism of the Catholic Church*, para. 1267.

3

# IS CHRISTIANITY BECOMING A CRIME?

> This article was written in response to "political correctness" and attempts to dumb-down the claim that ours is a Christian country.

Recently a parishioner gave me an article to read from one of our national newspapers entitled "How Britain is turning Christianity into a crime". They were understandably concerned about the situation it highlighted. The article cited several examples of what is basically "political correctness" gone berserk, incidents of people simply exercising their freedom of expression in the area of their Christian beliefs only to find themselves threatened with legal proceedings on the grounds that they were acting against religious or cultural "diversity". The most absurd example of this is certain local authorities banning public activities connected with Christmas on the grounds that they are 'too Christian'!

There was also the airline check-in lady who was disciplined (at the behest of the PC brigade) and threatened with the sack for wearing a small cross round her neck and yet, not very long afterwards, a court defended the right of a Hindu schoolgirl to wear a religious bangle (despite it contravening the uniform code of her school, a code she presumably accepted when she applied to go there). More recently we had the case of the nurse who was sacked for offering to pray with a patient, a request which apparently hadn't offended the elderly lady patient concerned, but which was reported by a colleague and then the PC brigade stepped in. And so it goes on.

Until just a few years ago the governing bodies of church schools were supported in law in their right to draw up admissions policies that allowed them to safeguard the religious character of their schools. The PC-ers and no small number of our politicians claimed this was a discriminatory practice – which is absurd. Yes, priority may have been given to Anglican, Catholic, etcetera, pupils at application, but it is primarily for them that these schools exist and they are part-financed through their respective churches. All other applicants were welcome after places were found for the pupils of the particular faith community concerned. In fact, typically, parents of (for example) Hindu and Muslim children have always wanted their children to attend church schools because of the excellence of the general education they receive there and the discipline that is enforced, and they were always welcome if places were available.

More recent legislation has systematically removed any such control over admissions policies in a deliberate attempt by PC-driven government to support multiculturalism and *diversity* – another thorn in the flesh of common sense. As a result church schools now struggle to educate their pupils in the area of faith because that is felt to be exclusive and against diversity. It has also become increasingly difficult to schedule RE classes in a specific Christian religion within the tight constraints of a national curriculum that supports only an all-inclusive study of comparative religions. In a twist to the doctrine in George Orwell's *Animal Farm* that "all animals are equal, but some are more equal than others", in this country all religions (and no religions) are equal, but Christianity, it would seem, is *less* equal than others.

Returning to the article we began with, the writer made a number of very telling points:

- Christianity is still the official religion of this country. All its institutions, its history and its culture are suffused with it; Britain would lose its identity, its values and its cohesion without it. But minority rights are now being wielded against it like a wrecking ball.

- Behaviour which was previously considered to transgress the moral norms of the Bible has now instead become the norm – and it is biblical values that are treated as beyond the pale of acceptable behaviour. Christianity has been dethroned as this country's governing creed on the basis that equality demands equal status for minority faiths and secularism.

- It is a process before which the Church of England has long been on its knees, going with the flow of moral and cultural collapse…and then wondering why its churches are so empty while those of uncompromising evangelicals are packed to the rafters.[1]
- The "sacred doctrine" of human rights – which explicitly sets itself up as the religion for a godless age – is the means by which secularism is steadily attacking the Christian roots of our civilisation.

It went on to cite Norfolk County Council objecting to the inclusion of the word "Christian" in the constitution of Barnabas House in King's Lynn which houses homeless young men; two Lancashire pensioners being interrogated by police for nearly an hour and a half about their homophobic views after they had merely asked their local council to display Christian literature alongside gay rights leaflets in civic buildings; Christian voluntary groups going out of existence when government funding is refused on the grounds that to be Christian means they are not committed to diversity; and Prince Charles' statement that when he becomes king (and as such Head of the Church of England) he no longer wishes to be called "Defender of the Faith" but the more inclusive "defender of faith".

We certainly used to be a Christian country and many have paid the ultimate price in defence of that claim, and statistically it would still seem to be the case, or at least nominally so. The 2001 census showed that 70% of the population declared themselves to be Christian; 3.5% of other faiths; 15% of no faith, and the remainder presumably didn't respond at all. If the newspaper article is accurate in the picture it presents and the questions it asks, it would seem that the 70% of us who claim to be Christian are simply not "fighting our corner". In effect we are apologising for our faith ("silence is taken as consent") ("decisions are taken by those who show up") and allowing our belief in God, and our freedom to bear witness to that faith, to be increasingly sidelined by a tide of political correctness and secularism from which God is missing.

Before I became a priest I lived and worked in Saudi Arabia for seven years, a country notorious for, as we would see it, the repressive nature of certain aspects of its social structures. One of those is the total and absolute ban on any religion other than Islam. That never stopped me from having some very positive and informative discussions with Saudi colleagues on our respective beliefs. We weren't out to convert one another, merely to better understand the faith we each professed. They would never have dreamt of reporting me to the authorities – we weren't in conflict, I wasn't threatening their religious freedoms nor criticising their beliefs – it was simply healthy and educational dialogue even within an otherwise very controlling society. With all due respect to them, and whilst not for a moment defending certain aspects of that theocracy (government based on religious beliefs), they do at least have the courage of their faith convictions, which is something we seem to be increasingly lacking.

Whether our country continues to be Christian will be defined by the faith commitment and practice of the majority of its citizens. This doesn't infer, nor should it result in, discrimination against any other religion (or those of no religion) whose rights and freedoms are implicit in the religious tolerance of our society[2] and don't need to be (super)imposed on us in the name of "political correctness" or diversity. The article is quite right in saying that secularism is steadily attacking the Christian roots of our civilisation – the biggest threat coming not from other faiths but from that part of our society that has no faith. We need to fight our corner. The trouble is we are British and we don't like to make a fuss and the same seems to be true of defending our religious beliefs. When I was a lay-missionary in Zambia, it was said that no soldier was ever issued with a megaphone because, given the ever-present threat of a military coup, everyone would follow the person with the loudest voice and that should belong to the President. Circumstances seem to be proving that, as Christians, we need to speak up a little, even a lot; our voice is currently nowhere near loud enough.

In his document on evangelisation[3], Pope Paul VI said:

> The faith in these days has often to contend with *secularism* or even atheism… We are speaking here of secularism strictly so-called, that is the conception of the world according to which it is entirely self-explanatory without any reference to God, who thus becomes unnecessary and is, as it were, an embarrassment. Secularism of this kind in seeking to assert the power of man, leads to a situation in which God is ignored or even denied…. The faith is challenged and threatened. Indeed it is often assailed and actively opposed. There is a danger therefore that it may either be overwhelmed by these attacks or starved for want of spiritual nourishment unless it is constantly fed and supported. Evangelisation therefore requires that the faithful be constantly provided with this nourishment and support for their faith.

We really do need to fight our corner and the last word on this is Our Lord's:

*In the world you will have trouble, but be brave:*
*I have conquered the world.*
(Jn 16:33)

*You are Peter and on this rock I will build my Church.*
*And the gates of the underworld can never*
*hold out against it.*
(Mt 16:18)

*Do not be afraid; only have faith.*
(Mk 5:36)

NOTES

1 In this respect we might have similar concerns to those of the Church of England.

2 We have hopefully learned our lesson from the dark days of the Reformation and the crusades.
3 *Evangelii nuntiandi* (8 December 1975).
4 In this respect we might have similar concerns to those of the Church of England.
5 We have hopefully learned our lesson from the dark days of the Reformation and the crusades.
6 Evangelii nuntiandi (8 December 1975).

4

# LIVING TOGETHER – LIVING APART

> An invitation to couples living together to consider putting their situation right as the Church sees it. Also some important pastoral information with regard to the sacraments for people who are separated or divorced.

Catholic couples, or couples where one partner is Catholic, seem to be living together without being married in about the same proportion as in society in general. It wouldn't be honest of me to say that, as a priest, the situation doesn't bother me, but that doesn't mean I'm going to be critical or judgmental. I'm not even going to say they are "living in sin" because, as I'll explain in a moment, that may not necessarily be the case. It's not an easy subject to address, and I certainly don't want to offend anyone. Rather what I hope to do is to offer a pastoral invitation to such couples to consider a more spiritually positive alternative for the future.

So, let's get the bad news out of the way first (there is also good news – later). We can't ignore either God's law or the Church's teaching on the subject of a physical relationship outside of marriage. Unfortunately the Church seems to prefer a low-key pastoral approach rather than a moral teaching approach to the situation of so many couples living together, with the result that little seems to be said publicly on the subject. That's all very well except that people begin to interpret the apparent silence as approval and, little by little, the impression is given that the standards that are increasingly acceptable in our society are also acceptable to the Church, whereas that isn't in fact the case. Regardless of what everyone else says is OK, as followers of Christ our bottom line is God's law and what *he* says is right and wrong.

On the other hand it may not always be correct to label couples living together as "living in sin". In order to commit sin we have to know that what we are doing is morally wrong and therefore sinful. If we don't in fact know, then our choice can't be sinful. The question is however: *should* we know? Have we failed to find out? – a point I'll come back to in a moment. I'm not at all convinced that Catholic young people these days are as informed as they should be on the moral teachings of the Church – either because we priests have avoided the subject, afraid that we might drive them away, or because their religious education in school (if they even attended Catholic schools) has been woefully lacking in those areas compared to the message they receive from their peers and from society. At the same time, if they experience only token practice of the faith at home – the primary source of their spiritual education – how can they possibly know?

There is also a question of whether, on a spiritual and sacramental level, couples realise that by living together, and presumably therefore being in a physical relationship, they exclude themselves from receiving Holy Communion. I'm not convinced that they do – given the answer of many of those who are asked the question and how often priests (who don't know it's happening) are asked by people (who do) why certain individuals in such relationships are still going up to receive the sacrament. Again this may simply be because they are not aware that their domestic situation is morally wrong in the eyes of God and the Church, or it may be because they have decided "in conscience" that it isn't in fact wrong. We are obliged to inform our conscience but that is a much more involved process than doing something because we feel it's right. We have to consider God's law and the Church's moral teaching, and possibly also seek guidance from our priest, so that we can be sure that the decision we then make before God is truly made in conscience.

Call me old fashioned, but whatever happened to engagements and abstinence? An engagement used to be an often lengthy period of time during which two people got to know each other socially, emotionally and every other "-ally" except physically. People didn't have to be actually living together in order to establish the foundations of a lasting relationship. These days, for all the living together that people do, the coming apart rate would suggest that particular choice doesn't seem to offer any firm guarantees. Why, then, are people choosing to live together, even to start a family together, without getting married? Why does marriage seem to be a "bridge too far"?

Possibly it's because it doesn't involve any long-term commitment in the way that marriage does. If something goes wrong, partners can walk out on the arrangement at any time – and many do. But what does that say about the attitude (not to mention the love) that a person brings with them into the relationship if there isn't the willingness to make a long-term commitment to the other person? It's wanting your cake and eating it. And what about any children there may be? Surely they deserve much better in terms of on-going love, security and stability. That's what marriage is all about after all: family – the building blocks of our society. If couples feel they can provide all of that whether they are married or not, then from a spiritual and pastoral point of view as Catholics, why not get married? Again, why is marriage a "bridge too far"?

As I said earlier, my intention in mentioning all of this isn't to criticise but to invite. Have couples who are living together thought about the spiritual and pastoral difficulties they are creating for themselves and in bringing up their children in the practice of the faith and being able to accompany them in their sacramental journey? I would want to ask whether there is any way they might consider putting things right – as God sees it and as the Church sees it – meeting with a priest to see what can be done, taking that extra step of commitment (within the sacrament of matrimony) to that other person in their life and to any children they may have? The possibilities are only a phone call away. That's the good news.

## Separated or divorced?

As we know, the Church doesn't accept civil divorce as an end to the vowed commitment of marriage made "'til death (not the courts) do us part". However the Church does, of course, accept the sad reality that sometimes, for whatever reasons, a relationship can break down irredeemably and irreconcilably and the only practical alternative is separation.

Many Catholics mistakenly believe that because they are separated, or their spouse has obtained a civil divorce, that they are no longer able to receive Holy Communion. This is not the case. Being separated or "divorced" (as the courts see it) doesn't in itself exclude a person from the sacraments. Whatever brought an end to the marriage may not even have been their fault. They may well have been the victim of circumstances beyond their control and are now living with the consequences of an action taken by their spouse. But if someone does feel responsible for the breakdown of their marriage, that is perhaps something that can be taken care of within the sacrament of confession.

What *could* exclude someone from receiving Holy Communion is if they have now entered into a second, and physical, relationship. The Church calls this "irregular" because it is morally unacceptable given that, in the eyes of the Church, the first marriage still exists. If they are simply living together the solution to the problem is clear, though it may not be a popular one, and that is for them to live apart and any physical involvement to end. But if there are children from that second relationship, or if they have made it legal by marrying again in a registry office or another church, then things are a little more difficult (possibly even impossible) to resolve.

Obtaining an annulment of the first marriage may be a possibility – so paving the way to resolving the second – though the annulment process can be complex and lengthy and offers no guarantees. The first step would be to speak to your parish priest; if you don't ask you will never find out.

It may be that, as things stand, there is no immediate or ready answer by which a return to the sacraments is possible – and this is a cause of very real pain to the Church and, no doubt, to the individuals concerned. The Church might wish it could simply wave a magic wand that would put things right, but it can't, any more than the couple can turn back the clock if they wished. The sad reality is that people make certain choices – perhaps in haste, perhaps under social or economic pressure – and only later do some of the more unfortunate consequences of those choices become apparent. What the Church wants them to know is that they are always welcome whenever their faith community gathers and that they are invited to come forward at Communion time to ask a blessing – not a blessing in the sense of approval of their situation, but a blessing in their "woundedness" as fellow members of the body of Christ. Bishop Crowley once said: *The only qualification that any of us needs for worshipping at Mass with the rest of our Catholic family is our faith in God and the need to express that faith in praise and adoration. If virtue or sinlessness were necessary requirements, not one of us would qualify!* He went on to urge each of us to ensure that our parish family always provides a welcome for any and all of its members.

The bottom line is that if you are separated or "divorced" but are not in a second (and physical) relationship, then there is nothing (apart from the usual needs that we all have for recourse to the sacrament of confession) to prevent you receiving Holy Communion. I wonder how many people are unnecessarily excluding themselves from the sacrament simply as a result of wrong information that they've been told, or have picked up? If in doubt, please ask (a priest).

5

## A PILGRIM PEOPLE – "FOLLOW ME"

> This article discusses the need to trust in the guidance of the Holy Spirit as the Church moves forward in its journey of faith, as opposed to the rather sad alternative of remaining anchored in the past.

Thomas said to Jesus, "Lord, we do not know where you are going, so how can we know the way?" to which Jesus replied, "I am the Way, the Truth and the Life." If we are truly followers of Jesus, then we have to believe not only that he is in charge of our faith journey, but that he has already taken the road that we are on.

Do they still have mystery tours? They used to have them from Redcar (where I grew up) and they always seemed to end up in Whitby for fish and chips and a stop at a pub on the way back. There was never much mystery to them, but people enjoyed the day out and that's what it was all about. Much of our day-to-day journey doesn't involve much mystery, or even much excitement, because we are familiar with the paths we are on. However, sometimes Jesus invites us somewhere new, to experience something different, and why wouldn't we want to follow where he leads? "But we've always done it this way" is a bit of a sad reason for doing anything and a particularly sad reason for not being open to change and new experiences in our relationship with God.

One of the new Eucharistic Prayers says: *With mighty hand and outstretched arm you led your people, Israel, through the desert. By the power of the Holy Spirit you guide your pilgrim Church today as it journeys along the paths of time to the eternal joy of your kingdom.* Let's just think for a moment about anchors and the difference between a regular anchor and a sea anchor. A regular anchor is a heavy object attached to a vessel and designed, when cast overboard, to grip the seabed and hold the boat or ship firmly in place. A sea anchor, on the other hand, is a canvas cone that floats out behind a vessel to help maintain a heading into the wind and prevent it drifting off course. One of the images of the Holy Spirit in scripture is that of wind and if we truly believe that the Spirit is at work in the Church, then we have to be open to following where the Spirit leads. We can't remain rooted in the past but must be open to the "wind" and "sea anchor" of the Spirit driving us forward but at the same time holding us firmly on course.

Those of us who are old enough to remember pre-Vatican II days, may recall them as a time when being a Catholic seemed so much easier. All we had to do was keep the commandments, show up for Mass on Sundays and holydays, go to Confession and Communion once a year "at Easter or thereabouts" and that was that, home and dry – or so we thought. Then along came the Second Vatican Council and all of a sudden being a Catholic seemed a lot more demanding because the practice of our faith was no longer simply about *doing* but is now also about *being*. Many people saw the changes as a whole new journey rather than being a slight change of course in the same journey they were already on. And instead of trusting that the Holy Spirit was guiding the Church just as surely as ever, the invitation to change and growth and new experience was rejected. We are always travelling in and with the Spirit and if we don't or can't accept that, then how can we be people of faith? Sadly, forty-five years after the Council, there are still people anchored in the past. The saddest thing of all is that, in a sense, the ship of their faith sailed without them and they may no longer know how to get back on board even if they wanted to.

Being on board means being a pilgrim because, like it or not, the Church is on a journey, always on the move. Being on the move infers change but change doesn't always sit too well because we become comfortable with what is familiar. And yet our world and our lives are always changing. Even though we may think that a great deal has changed in the Church over the course of our lifetime (because we have personally experienced it), things haven't really changed very much at all. Through the ages the Church has adapted the way it has preached the gospel and it has also embraced aspects of the various cultures in which the seed of the Church has been planted. If it hadn't, it might still be a minority sect worshipping on the shores of the Sea of Galilee and not the worldwide religion it has become. However, the essence of the Church – that which is at its very core and which makes it what it is – hasn't really changed since Our Lord founded it two thousand years ago.

We can't dig our heels in and expect things to stay the same just because we don't like change. The Church isn't about you or me as individuals, it's about all of us together as members of the body of Christ. In our journey of faith we have got to trust the leadership and guidance of the Holy Spirit and be willing to go where Our Lord, through the Church, calls us to follow.

## Mobility and change

In the Old Testament, the tabernacle was the portable sanctuary that housed the Ark of the Covenant. By definition the word *tabernacle* means a portable dwelling, a tent, hence the tabernacle was also referred to as the Tent of Meeting, the place where God dwelt with his people, the physical sign of his presence with them. Wherever they journeyed in the desert, the Ark went with them and wherever they set up camp, the Tent of Meeting was set up and the Ark was housed there. This is, perhaps, the most helpful image we have of the concept of a pilgrim people, a people on a journey of faith following where God leads. There was no concept at the time of permanence, of settling down – that would happen only after God had led his people to the land he had promised to give them.

Jesus himself never established a single physical church in his life; rather he travelled round from place to place, preaching and teaching in the squares and market places and occasionally in existing synagogues. He met the people where they were, he ministered to them and then he moved on to the next town or village or city. And when he did establish his "church" on the "rock" of Peter and the disciples, their mission wasn't to set up physical places of worship, but to go out and preach the Good News to people everywhere – wherever they were.

There was a story a few years ago about a priest in Australia who had a small church built on a motorised barge which he could then take up and down the various rivers and creeks of his obviously quite extensive parish literally bringing church to the people wherever they were. Oh that we had such mobility and flexibility! Historically we have built our churches and cathedrals in brick and stone and they were built to last. But then if the population moves and they are no longer at the heart of the worshipping community, what can you do? Buildings can't be moved. Our encounter with Christ isn't limited to physical structures; wherever people are gathered in his name he will be there with them.

Even allowing for the emotional and spiritual attachment that people may have to what has been their parish church for a great many years, the reality is that churches are just bricks and mortar. I grew up in the Sacred Heart parish in Redcar and will always regard with fondness the church of my first sacraments. But Redcar grew and eventually a new parish (St Alban's) was established in the south of the town. As that was where I lived, I committed myself to support the development of this new faith community and in due course saw the new church open and that became my parish. Wherever I have subsequently lived and worked became "home" and the local church my parish and, of course, this has been especially true as a priest.

This need to be flexible and mobile in our affections, is especially important where parishes have to be amalgamated or where, sadly, churches have to be closed. Such decisions are not taken lightly and are usually an unavoidable response to a situation where church-going populations have either moved or numbers have fallen so dramatically that, practically and/or economically, formerly independent parish communities are no longer sustainable. Looking to the roots of the Eucharistic celebration that is at the heart of our faith communities – the Last Supper, it is always desirable that as many as possible should gather together in communion around the one table. We should therefore always welcome our churches being full as a result of amalgamation rather than being largely empty but independent.

6

# HALLOWEEN

> People seem to have become very blasé about some of the activities and symbols attached to Halloween. The intention of this pastoral reflection is to encourage them to be more realistic and more aware.

In an article in the *Yorkshire Post*, the Anglican Bishop of Bolton, the Rt Rev David Gillett, wrote:

> I share the view of many Christians that large retailers are increasingly keen to commercialise Halloween celebrations in a way that pressurises parents to purchase goods that promote the dark, negative side of Halloween. I am worried that [this] has the potential to trivialise the realities of evil and that occult practices should not be condoned, even if they are only being presented in a caricatured, light-hearted form. Those in the Church supporting a move towards a more positive approach to the event are not being killjoys, but are simply reflecting the concerns of many parents and teachers across the land. The Church of England encourages Christians to celebrate All Saints' Day – the day after Halloween – with bright parties and it's high time we reclaimed the Christian aspects of Halloween.

I include this quote to show that I'm not the only one going on about Halloween. There are also several sites on the internet in which the same concerns are being expressed – especially by Christian contributors.

The word *Halloween* comes from *All Hallows' Even* – literally the evening before the celebration of "all the hallowed", all the saints of God, on November 1st, but trying to find a reliable and accurate explanation of where our modern Halloween practices came from is by no means easy.

Its origins are probably to be found in the fifth century Celtic pagan ceremoniesmarking their new year. It was a calendar celebration to do with the arrival of the dark days of winter, but it also had to do with the pagan belief that the spirits of those who had died during the year roamed about that night in search of a living body they could possess for the year ahead. So on the night of October 31st, people would make their homes as cold and unwelcoming as possible and parade around in frightening costumes to keep the spirits away. As the centuries passed people continued to dress up, specifically as hobgoblins, ghosts and witches, but perhaps without realising exactly why. The purpose of the turnip or pumpkin jack-o' lantern may also have been to frighten the spirits away. It also became common for pranks to be carried out as if done by the spirits – perhaps the origins of "mischief night" and "trick-or-treating".

With the establishment of the Christian calendar, October 31st became the eve of All Hallows (All Saints day) but had no other significance. So Hallow's Eve (or E'en) doesn't seem to have grown out of evil practices as such and therefore, if the name itself came from the Christian calendar, why has it now become associated as much as it has with devils and the even darker practices of Satanism, witchcraft and the occult? Indeed Halloween is a particularly significant date on the calendar for those involved in such practices – and there is a lot more of it about than most people realise. Part of the answer has to do with how commercialised Halloween has become and, as a consequence, people seeing it as just a harmless bit of fun, a classic example of *desensitisation* – failing to see things as they really are.

Let's take another example – that of Bonfire Night. Every year the whole country celebrates November 5th with bonfires and fireworks, but what exactly is being celebrated?

On the night of 5 November 1605, Guy Fawkes was arrested in the cellars of the Houses of Parliament where he was about to ignite a cache of gunpowder. Fawkes was a member – though not leader – of a gang of Catholics plotting the death of King James I and his Protestant parliament. Some of the gang escaped but Fawkes and others were arrested, tried and executed. Bonfires were lit across the land to celebrate the safety of the king, an action that became an annual celebration which continues to this day with the addition of burning an effigy of Guy Fawkes on those bonfires (even though he was hanged, not burned at the stake). What, though, are *we* doing when *we* celebrate Bonfire Night?

If it once was a celebration of the specific fact that Catholic plotters were caught and executed, the reality faded over the centuries and it became more a celebration of the fact that the plot never succeeded regardless of who the perpetrators were. However it just might make us pause and think whether as Catholics we should be celebrating the execution of Catholics, but then our sympathies shouldn't be with the plotters of such a murderous act whatever their religious motivation. Of course it does beg the question as to whether Bonfire Night is long-past its "best by" date anyway. Does a foiled plot really still have that much political significance that we continue to mark the date over four centuries later?

The point I am making is that we can become desensitised to the reality behind what we are doing – whether on Bonfire Night or, in this case, on Halloween – and the fact that what we are doing is actually driven and promoted solely by commercial interests.

When I was a kid, Halloween was an evening of harmless fun. We had already done "mischief night" on the 30th and therefore Halloween was only to do with turnip lanterns (pumpkins weren't really available) and dressing up as witches and ghosts – but nothing evil, nothing sinister. I suppose dressing as a witch was somewhat questionable come to think of it though, as kids, we probably only had the fairytale image in mind and certainly not the darker aspect of witchcraft. And ours were simple homemade costumes, not the modern mass-produced stuff, the sale of which (weeks beforehand) lines the pockets of our supermarkets and novelty shops.[1] The American practice of going door-to-door "trick-or-treating" had yet to cross the Atlantic we just played around in the street close to our homes trying to scare passers-by and other kids, and maybe telling one another ghost stories. Nowadays children are dressed up as monsters and, more worrying still, as devils

– where did that come from? Do parents ever stop to think what their children are doing, what they are *letting* them do?

During the baptismal rite, and during the renewal of baptismal promises at Easter, all present are asked: "Do you reject Satan? And all his works? And all his empty promises?" All who are serious about their Christian faith and their own baptismal promises answer emphatically "I do!" to each question. It can sometimes make the hairs on the back of your neck stand up because it is a very serious declaration and there is something very powerful about such a communal rejection of the devil and his works. In fact if the reply is mumbled I will often repeat the question until I get an appropriately convincing response! Why, then, on Halloween, do so many Christian parents allow their children to dress up as devils? Why do so many people participate in Halloween activities which, if not actually courting evil and occultism, walk a very thin line of association with those dark things that have no place in our lives as Christians?

Typically (and dismissively) people will say: "It's only a bit of fun" – fun for whom? Whose image is being promoted? Whose work may thereby be being done for him? Isn't it blurring the lines between good and evil for children? And, anyway, what do such things have to do with All Hallows and the celebration of the lives of the saints? Increasingly Christian denominations and church leaders are now speaking out, out of their concern for the sort of things that are typically a part of Halloween. Many offer Christian-based gatherings as an alternative activity, particularly for children. Can we not find other, and better, things to do given the reality that, when we get involved in that darker side of things, we are doing the devil's work for him by promoting his image? We really need to be more aware, more discerning, and to look at things more objectively.[2]

What acceptable alternatives are there?

Sadly, in this day and age, many traditional activities may not hold much appeal to children any more: things like apple-bobbing, making toffee and toffeeapples, carving turnip/pumpkin lanterns and so on. "Trick-or-treating" may be OK in harmless, fun costumes and where it doesn't cause a nuisance to others. (I know of elderly people who have suffered foul mouthed abuse from youngsters when they hadn't any sweets to give or because they refused to open their door at night.) For a number of reasons "trick-or-treating" isn't the safest of activities anyway these days. Most obvious is the fact of young children often being allowed to wander the streets at night without an accompanying adult. It has also been known for needles, pins and pieces of razor blade to be concealed in sweets and fruit being given to children. The obvious solution is to not let children go "trick-or-treating" in the first place[3], or to only allow them to go to the houses of trusted neighbours.

All things considered, perhaps it shouldn't be called Halloween anymore because, clearly, much of what goes on that night has nothing to do with it being the eve of All Saints, and what is meant to be holy has in many cases become decidedly unholy. But then, where does parental discernment come into the picture? If a parent wouldn't deliberately put their child at physical risk on Halloween, why wouldn't they also want to keep them from spiritual risk, teaching them about that blurred line between spiritual good and evil?

The saying has it that idle hands are the devil's playground. I wonder whether the same might be said of desensitisation when it dulls our awareness of the demands of our Christian faith and our Christian witness. We have to stand up and be counted and, if that ever seems a pain, we need only look to the cross and the pain Our Lord bore for us. As we have said, the baptismal rite asks: "Do you reject Satan? And all his works? And all his empty promises?" Hopefully a resounding "We do" is our answer to each of those questions, in which case please don't let your children dress up like him; don't get involved in things that have to do with his works and his efforts to persuade us that "it's only a bit of fun". Again, fun for whom? Whose image is being promoted? Whose work may thereby being done for him?

## NOTES

1 And just take a look at some of those costumes. What do they have to do with the eve of All Saints?

2 Manchester United, for example, has a red devil on its club badge and this has become the team's nickname. Most people don't even give the badge, or the name, a second thought which may be just as well given the international profile of the club and therefore the international promotion that image receives. But that's precisely the problem – people have lost sight of the reality.

3 Why do children even need to be "begging" door-to-door for sweets? – which is what it amounts to.

7

# WHERE ARE ALL THE PEOPLE?

An invitation to consider our shared call to the work of evangelisation and the suggestion that if we were carrying out that work as fully as perhaps we should be, then our churches might be a little fuller.

The *epiphany* process is firstly one of revelation – symbolised by the journey of the Magi to discover the Messiah, in itself a symbol of our own journey of faith as we come to an ever greater discovery of the person of Jesus Christ in our lives. But there is then a further stage to that process as we in turn respond to our Christian vocation to be witnesses to our faith, to be *epiphany* to others as we invite them to experience the reality and presence of Christ in their lives. This is what evangelisation is all about – being a prophet, spreading the Good News, spreading the word, bringing others to a knowledge of Christ, building up the kingdom, vitalising and (where necessary) *re*vitalising the body of Christ from within. That is our call from our baptism.

I think we therefore need to ask the question: where are all the people? To be sustainable, let alone evangelising, our parishes need people. For generations we have been baptising anyone and everyone who came knocking on the presbytery door; children automatically made their first Holy Communion in entire class groups as soon as they reached age seven; and the same was true of the sacrament of confirmation three years later. How many celebrated each of these sacraments with you? Where are they all now? Why are the pews relatively empty when they should be packed? Apparently the presence of Jesus Christ, the Son of God, on the altar under the appearance of bread and wine isn't interesting enough, not even miracle enough, to keep them in the practice of their faith. It has been the best of all possible reasons for two thousand years but not, apparently, for this generation. And avoiding mortal sin, as sad a reason as that is for not missing Mass, no longer seems to matter either. The concept of sin, and in particular serious sin, is no longer fashionable (apparently) and to even mention it is the height of political incorrectness (seemingly). Well, to the best of my knowledge neither the Church, nor God, has made any statement to that effect and so, as in the military, you go with the last order issued…and that would have been by God.

The word of God can sometimes be a bit of a challenge and, as a result, doesn't always sit too well with us. The New Testament book of Revelation records that in the vision he received from God, St John was handed a scroll to eat[1], a scroll that had the word of God written on the front and back. He was told that it would taste sweet as he ate it but that it would turn sour in his stomach. This is often how God's word is experienced – initially with enthusiasm but, later, a little less so when the consequences become more apparent. That was the experience of the young man in the gospel who approached Jesus to ask what he must do to inherit eternal life. He was keen enough to ask the question but afterwards he probably wished he hadn't because the answer he received from Jesus was, initially at least, too much of a challenge for him.

So where are all the people? Well, they are just not going to church anymore. But why? Typically, if you asked them, they would probably blame the Church but then they *are* the church, *we* are church, so is it our fault or is it perhaps their fault? Maybe it's not actually anyone's fault so much as it is a sign of the times as I was just saying.

I often think back to my school days and the old "penny catechism" much of which we had to learn by heart. It wasn't the best teaching method in the world, but we did at least know what was what. What are kids learning of their faith in Catholic schools today? I honestly don't know. They seem to know more about other faiths (political correctness again!) than they do about their own. I remarked to one youngster recently that I hadn't seen them at Mass for a while to which the answer was: "I've had a lot of homework"! The concept just wasn't there that we are supposed to be at Mass every Sunday and that that should be a priority.[2] There was certainly no concept of the fact that deliberately missing Mass is seriously (mortally) sinful and is a matter for confession before we receive Communion again. Is no one (parents, teachers, priests) teaching these things anymore?

It is a sad fact of life that there are people who have had very negative experiences of one sort or another that have alienated them from the Church. Such situations could hopefully be put right if parish priests were made aware of them but mind-reading was not on the curriculum at the seminary – someone has to tell us. As long as this continues not to happen, people are depriving themselves of the sacraments and that is a great sadness and one that could very easily be resolved. On the other hand, the vast majority of those who no longer go to church simply stopped going and have never started again and the more time that passes the harder it gets to put the situation right.

Do you know of such people? Could you (gently) approach them and find out whether there is anything that can be done? It doesn't matter how long they have been away, it doesn't even matter *why* they have been away, what does matter is that, as a faith community, we would like to welcome them back.

It's not just my job as a priest, indeed – as recent papal documents have consistently pointed out – it is more effectively your job because you know who these people are, they are your neighbours, you work with them, you see them in the shops, the café or the pub – and they may find your approach less "threatening" than that of a priest[3]. This, too, is evangelisation because it is bringing people a very special word of God that will hopefully encourage them back to the practice of their faith, build up the body of Christ, and make our faith community just that little bit more sustainable for the future.

## NOTES

1 It's a funny word, scroll. It always reminds me of that Morecambe & Wise sketch taking place in either Roman or Shakespearean times. Eric asks: Do you have the scrolls? and Eric answers: No, I always walk like this." Sorry, as I was saying…

2 Of course a further problem is that, unlike years ago, young children often have to rely on parents to take them to church these days and so if parents decide not to go then their children can't go.

3 Even a nice priest like me!

8

## A CONTINUUM OF PASTORAL CARE

> This article presents important information which Catholics should know about in the area of pastoral care of the sick, the dying and the bereaved.

What I would like to try to set out below is very important pastoral information which Catholics should know about in advance of any situation of need. It is often very difficult to try to explain reasons why and why not in this area when people are upset or bereaved and emotions are understandably high.

In 1972, Pope Paul VI authorised a new rite for the anointing of the sick which replaced the earlier rite. Following officially approval, the English text – Pastoral Care of the Sick – was published for use in this country in 1983. As we will see in a moment, the new Sacrament of the Sick (in its fullest form Communion and anointing – for the sick not just for the dying) continues to be associated in people's minds with the old "last rites", which not only does a disservice to the sacrament, but can sometimes make pastoral care of the sick unnecessarily difficult for the priest.

Two years before that, a new rite for funerals had also been authorised. Once again the English text took a little time to be approved officially, but the Order of Christian Funerals was eventually published by our Bishops' Conference in 1990 and its use made mandatory from Easter Sunday 1991. The two rites taken together provide what was referred to in our seminary studies as a "continuum of care", a pastoral provision that becomes clearer when we look at the component parts of the two texts.

The text for the pastoral care of the sick begins with prayers to be offered when making such a visit – not even a Eucharistic visit but simply one made out of pastoral concern and to offer the support and encouragement of scripture and prayer. There is then a longer rite to be used in visiting someone who may be confined to home or a hospital for a long enough period of time that a Eucharistic visit becomes appropriate, whether made by a priest, deacon or minister of Holy Communion.

The rite then provides for the anointing of the sick (which can take place within, or outside of, Mass). The introduction explains that the purpose of this sacrament is to offer encouragement, hope and support to those whose health is seriously impaired by sickness or old age. It may also be celebrated with someone who is about to undergo treatment or surgery in hospital and it may be repeated if, for example, the person recovers and then becomes ill again, or if, during the same illness, their condition becomes more serious.

Being anointed with the Oil of the Sick is the principal action and sign of the sacrament, a sacrament celebrated with someone who is sick and not necessarily dying. Therefore it is extremely important that people no longer associate being anointed with what used to be called "the last rites" when a priest was typically called at the last moment to anoint someone on the point of death or, as used to happen, actually anointing them after they had died. That's not what the sacrament of the sick is about. A priest should be able to visit someone who is sick at home or in hospital, to celebrate the sacrament with them, without causing them to panic – which they will if they continue to associate being anointed with being given the "last rites". In this context oil is a symbol of renewal and new life (we use oil in various forms to, for example, enrich wooden surfaces, restore life to leather, and to treat dry skin).

On the other hand, and perhaps contrary to earlier practice, the priority for someone who is approaching death is for them to receive the sacrament of Holy Communion, not just to be anointed. This introduces the word viaticum which, in its literal sense, means "food for the journey": Holy Communion as spiritual nourishment for the passage through death to eternal life.

As the rite points out, if someone has been anointed at the beginning of a serious illness, viaticum (Communion) received when death is close, will be better understood as the last sacrament of Christian life: viaticum, not anointing. It is important, therefore, that a request to receive Communion should be made when the person is still able to receive and to participate as fully as possible in the rite. Viaticum may be received frequently, even daily. The person may then also be anointed, although in this case the sign and action is meant to offer hope, support and encouragement as death approaches. In this context a phrase may be used that we were familiar with in the old rite: extreme unction or final anointing. Communion as viaticum is always a priority unless circumstances make it impossible. If the person is unable to receive, or if it the priest has been called to an emergency situation where there is no opportunity for Communion, the priest should then anoint them and give absolution.

In terms of what we have called a "continuum of care", the rite then provides prayers and readings for when death has occurred. It is very important to bear in mind that a priest is not permitted to anoint someone after they have died and therefore shouldn't be put on the spot by being asked to do so. As the text of the rite states:

> A priest is not to administer the sacraments of penance or anointing, instead he should pray for the dead person. It may be necessary to explain to the family that sacraments are celebrated for the living, not for the dead, and that the dead are (more) effectively helped by the prayers of the living.

During the Prayers for the Dead, the priest may make the sign of the cross on the forehead of the deceased and/or bless their body with holy water, but he may not anoint them. Given that immediately after death is not the best time to try to explain this to family members who may not know and have asked for the person to be anointed, we priests need to keep repeating the Church's teaching so that people do know. Another point to be borne in mind is that the Prayers for the Dead are intended to be said with family members present, as much for their support and consolation as for the person who has died. This is confirmed in the text by such phrases as *it may be necessary to explain to the family, the minister greets those who are present,* and that the body may be blessed *for the comfort of those present.*

*

Pastoral care and pastoral need following a death now take us on to the second of the texts, the *Order of Christian Funerals* with its options for the various funeral rites that can be celebrated – again decisions that should be made in discussion with the parish priest, not the funeral director.

The text continues where the other left off, providing prayers to be said with the family in the presence of the deceased whether immediately after death or later at home or in a chapel of rest. It then offers various options according to what the family decides, decisions which, again, should be made after discussion with the priest.

The first option is for the deceased to be received into church the night before the funeral. This was often an almost automatic choice, but it happens less and less these days. The extra cost involved may be a consideration, also a church's remote location may make it inadvisable to leave a coffin unattended overnight. It also has to be said that a reception can be as upsetting for a family as the funeral itself and they perhaps need to consider whether they are going to be able to handle the double upset of a reception and then the funeral itself.

The next decision to be taken is whether it is to be a funeral service or a funeral (requiem) Mass. As the text states:

> The Order of Christian Funerals makes provision for the minister, in consultation with the family, to choose those rites and texts that are most suitable to the situation (and) most closely apply to the needs of the mourners.

When the deceased has made a specific request in this regard then, obviously, as far as possible this must be respected, but this in itself highlights all the more the need for decisions to be made together as a family ahead of time – preferably when death isn't imminent and therefore decisions can be made in light of practical, not purely emotional, considerations.

A funeral is our cultural way of bidding farewell to someone who has died and of then disposing of their mortal remains in a way that hopefully offers comfort and consolation to the bereaved. In that sense, therefore, the rites that accompany the funeral are for the benefit of the bereaved. In an ideal situation, where the entire family is church-going, the Church would envisage requiem Mass being the automatic choice. However such an ideal is increasingly rare these days and it might, therefore, be unhelpful to make family members sit through a funeral Mass if, because they no longer practise their faith, they would therefore be excluded from the sacrament of Communion which is at the heart of the celebration. Mass for the deceased can be offered at any time, and so the more immediate question is what funeral rite will be most supportive and consoling for the immediate family? These are things that, again, should be discussed ahead of time, and which need to be discussed with the priest before any other arrangements are made with the funeral director.

On the sometimes difficult subject of choosing songs and music, the Order says that the texts of the songs chosen should express the paschal mystery of the Lord's suffering, death and triumph over death and should be related to the readings from Scripture. We are therefore not allowed to use secular music in church, though occasionally a piece of classical instrumental music might be appropriate.

The rite reminds us that scripture readings may not be replaced by non-biblical readings (an appropriate short poem may be read by a family member or friend in addition to the readings from scripture) and that liturgical tradition assigns the proclamation of the readings to readers [commissioned ministers of the word] as opposed to family members or friends being asked to read. It may be more appropriate for one of them to be asked to say a few words about the deceased – if they felt they'd be able to on the day.

As far as the committal is concerned, burial has long been traditional for Catholics although the Church does now permit cremation where at one time it didn't. Once again this is best discussed as a family ahead of time. Someone saying they want to be cremated is all very well; it's whether the immediate family is OK with such a choice that matters. The rite provides a short service of committal for use at the graveside, or at the crematorium, as well as for the burial or dispersal of ashes.

Whilst fully acknowledging the grief of the bereaved and the loss they have suffered, the focus of a Christian funeral is on the future: on life after death. We gather to worship in hope of resurrection – that's what our Christian faith is all about. At the same time, of course, we are also celebrating and thanking God for the life of the person who has died. The funeral rites seek to achieve a balance between these various aspects and, in their own way, conclude the continuum of spiritual and pastoral care that has gone before.

9

# CLERICALISM V ACCOUNTABILITY

> In some respects this article would make good reading for the clergy, but my purpose was to explain to lay people the extent to which priests, as stewards, should be accountable to them.

What is clericalism? The dictionary says it's *a policy of supporting the power or influence of the clergy in secular matters, or of maintaining or increasing the power of a religious hierarchy.* Either definition should give cause for concern. Generally the word is used to refer to deference or privilege either being given to a priest, or being assumed by a priest, solely because he *is* a priest – as if the words "ordination" and "elevation" were somehow interchangeable! There is also a tendency for people to put priests on a pedestal whether they like it or not and whether they deserve it or not.[1] Some examples:

It's bad enough when, at a parish function, people in line for food or a drink will insist that, as a priest, you go ahead of them, but it's worse still when you see priests automatically walk to the front of the line as if they have a right as a priest (whatever that means) to do so – a clerical right. On one level that's clericalism.

Another example would be people giving deference to the opinion of a priest because he's a priest when, in fact, he may have no knowledge or expertise whatsoever on the subject in question. It's even worse when the priest himself insists on his opinion, refusing all other advice, because he's the priest. That's clericalism too.

Of course it can also work the other way. It will be reported to the priest that, let's say, a toilet is running over or an outside drain is blocked, as if "Father" is the only one who can fix these things. He isn't. That can be convenient clericalism!

The priest can't have it both ways. There's a danger that a priest who effectively insulates himself in his "clerical tower" can become a law unto himself, feeling he is accountable to, and responsible only for, himself. As unfortunate as such a situation might be, if that is his choice then he only has himself to blame if the people leave everything for him to do.

Both the definitions above use the word "power" and the last thing the priesthood should be is a power trip. What it may involve is "authority" but that is a very different thing to power, though it too can be used wrongly.

The various definitions of power include words like "ability" and "capacity" – someone may have power but what is important is their ability, their capacity, to exercise well the authority that their position gives them. The word "authority" itself implies having a right to act or decide or judge, but doing so from a base of knowledge or experience or belief. And so any power or authority that a priest may have isn't to be wielded autocratically. It should be accorded to him by the people to whom he ministers on the basis that his ministry reflects knowledge, experience and conviction. Vocation to priesthood comes from God and ministry is founded on that call. When Pilate said to Jesus, 'Surely you know I have the power to release you and I have the power to crucify you?' his reply was, 'You would have no power over me if it had not been given you from above.' Food for priestly thought.

## Accountability?

At his priestly ordination, the candidate is asked by his bishop:

> Are you resolved, with the help of the Holy Spirit, to discharge without fail the office of priesthood in the presbyterial order as a conscientious fellow worker with your bishop in caring for the Lord's flock?
>
> Are you resolved to celebrate the mysteries of Christ faithfully and religiously as the Church has handed them down to us, for the glory of God and the sanctification of Christ's people?

> Are you resolved to exercise the ministry of the word worthily and wisely, preaching the Gospel and explaining the Catholic faith?
>
> Are you resolved to consecrate your life to God for the salvation of his people, and to unite yourself more closely every day to Christ the High Priest, who offered himself for us to the Father as a perfect sacrifice?

A priest is accountable first and foremost to God but he puts that into practice principally through his accountability to his bishop. That is the commitment contained in the first of those questions, a commitment renewed annually at the Chrism Mass. But he is also accountable to the people to whom he ministers, as those other questions make clear, a commitment also renewed annually.

How someone exercises his priesthood is perhaps a measure of how seriously he takes his responsibilities and accepts his accountability. Of course some aspects of this may not always sit too well with the people, especially those who may prefer a quiet life to being taught and challenged. What is it they say: "Every ship is safer in harbour, but that's not what ships are for"? And then there's that saying about Jesus, something to the effect that he comforted the challenged and challenged the comfortable. If we truly share Our Lord's own ministry then that's what we priests have to do also – even when it involves risk. Realistically we can't please all of the people all of the time, but we do have to please God all of the time. Again, though, priests can't do that from a position of power nor can they do it on their own.

In an ideal world the call to priesthood would come "from the people for the people" – from God, yes, but a person identified by the community and called into priestly service of that community. Sadly, however, things don't work that way and, heeding perhaps Our Lord's own caution that a prophet is never accepted in his own country, priests are usually appointed anywhere other than to their home parishes.

If we did have "home-grown" priests in that sense, they would be much more aware of and sensitive to the history of the community and of its church. As things are, in many ways a priest is a "passing guest" and yet that can't become an excuse for not investing himself or his energies in a parish simply because he won't be there for ever, any more than it can be an excuse for people detaching themselves from his spiritual leadership for the same reason.

Certainly in the case of long-established parishes, many families will have lived there for years, perhaps their whole lives. In every sense of the word it is *their* parish – they have grown up in it, they have supported it, they have celebrated their sacraments in it and it's where they worship week in, week out. Every once in a while they will lose their priest and a new one will arrive and before long he may start changing this and moving that and doing things differently. I can sympathise with people who find it unsettling and perhaps resent what they see as interference by a newcomer. However, from the moment a priest arrives it becomes *his* parish also, and if he didn't feel at home or consider the parish to be his home, questions ought to be asked – of the people and of him.

Liturgical changes often require structural changes and that's why altars were brought forward and pulpits disappeared, fonts were relocated and altar rails were removed – it wasn't just the whim of the priest. Change and adaptation continue to be necessary from time to time but because change is never very popular, the priest who has to carry it out risks upsetting people even though that isn't his intention. It would certainly help the situation if he explained things to the people and why he would like to make the changes in question, perhaps in particular discussing things with the Parish Council. It's all part of that same aspect of accountability and responsibility that we just talked about. A priest must lead, must do what he feels to be right and good for the majority, and must do and teach what the Church says must be done and taught, otherwise he is useless to the people.

Things can't stay the way they've always been – we are members of a pilgrim church, a church on the move, and while we may not always be happy with change we do have to trust in the direction and guidance of the Holy Spirit and respond generously to the spiritual growth and development that the Spirit brings about. It's in our Creed – "I believe in the Holy Spirit, the Lord and giver of *life*". And it's the priest's responsibility to challenge the people spiritually and to invite them forward in their pilgrimage of faith. If he fails to do that, settling instead for a quiet life, then he will be just like the man in the gospel parable who took his one talent and buried it for safe keeping – and we all know what happened to him when his master called him to account. Jesus himself told that story, so we can't ignore its implications just because we aren't comfortable with them. But it's amazing how often people do exactly that, choosing to ignore the teaching of the priest and holding instead to their own (often outdated) ideas and practices. "He's only the priest, what does he know?" What's wrong with that picture?

This is perhaps the positive face of clericalism – a priest's legitimate efforts on behalf of the people because he is the priest, *their* priest. It's what the bishop sent him to do, that's what God calls him to do, and so that's what he does. But it's not about power, it's about invitation; and it's not about autocracy, it's about co-operation. In that sense there should be accountability in the other direction: that the people of a parish be accountable to their priest for the degree to which they trust and follow his pastoral and spiritual leadership and by their involvement in all aspects of their shared parish life.

*Jesus said: 'I am the good shepherd;*
*the good shepherd is one*
*who lays down his life for his sheep.*
*The hired man, since he is not the shepherd*
*and the sheep do not belong to him,*
*abandons the sheep and runs away*
*as soon as he sees a wolf coming*
*because he is only a hired man*
*and has no concern for the sheep.*

(Jn 10:11-13)

NOTE

1 It's too easy to fall off a pedestal and it can be a long drop!

10

# COMMUNION UNDER BOTH KINDS

A pastoral invitation, especially to those who receive only the host, to consider experiencing the fullness of the sacrament.

Back in December 2005, Bishop Crowley wrote to the priests of his diocese expressing concern at the fact that Communion under both kinds was not being offered in some parishes and reminding us that "Communion under both kinds is certainly the mind of the Church and very much the desire of our own Bishops' Conference". Despite this, people still point to the Church's teaching that we receive the fullness of the sacrament even if we receive only the consecrated host. On the surface it might appear that the Church is teaching two contradictory approaches to the sacrament, but this is not, of course, the case and this becomes clear if we take a look at what is actually being said.

The catechism teaches (para. 1390):

> Since Christ is sacramentally present under each of the species[1], Communion under the species of bread alone makes it possible to receive all the fruit of Eucharistic grace.

But it then goes on:

> For pastoral reasons this manner of receiving Communion has been legitimately established as the most common form in the Latin rite. But the sign of Communion is more complete when given under both kinds, since in that form the sign of the Eucharistic meal appears more clearly.

Two distinct things are being said here – one concerning the spiritual aspect of the sacrament and the other concerning the physical sign, and a key phrase in that second section from the catechism is "for pastoral reasons", referring to why people began to receive the host only in the first place.

One of the biggest obstacles to our understanding and reception of Holy Communion is history. For a long time in our recent past, the majority of people at Mass didn't receive Communion at all – which makes as much sense as going to a restaurant, spending an hour studying the menu, and then deciding not to eat! This habit of non-reception (or at least only annual reception at Easter) probably resulted from a number of factors: the requirement at the time that we had to fast from midnight; a close connection being made between Confession and Communion such that people felt they couldn't go to Communion unless they had been to confession first; and possibly also a feeling that we were unworthy to receive Communion frequently. What was lost was the practice instituted by Jesus at the Last Supper when he blessed and gave his disciples both bread and wine, both his body and blood – that's how the sacrament was supposed to be received, and that's how it *was* received for the first ten centuries of the Church.

Little by little, regular reception of Communion became more commonplace once again, but still only under one kind – the host – supported by Church teaching that that was sufficient to receive the fullness of the graces of the sacrament. But that is not what Our Lord intended, otherwise he would not have offered his disciples both bread and wine. When, in 1970, the Church once again permitted the chalice to be offered to everyone, the theology of those centuries should also have been updated in order to ensure that the sacrament would now be received in its fullest form once again (except, of course, by those unable to tolerate alcohol or the taste of wine).

The physical elements of bread and wine (consecrated to the body and blood of Christ) are the signs and symbols of the sacrament in its fullness, helping us to recognise and experience who and what it is we are receiving. Yes the Church says that we still have that option, but why would we want it? Why would someone not want to receive the fullness of the sacrament by participating in it in the fullest possible way (unless, again, they have an intolerance to wine or its taste)? 1970 should have been a time of great rejoicing amongst Catholics as we were permitted once again to receive Communion as it was meant to be received – under both kinds. Instead, nearly forty years later, we still have people walking past the chalice, walking past Jesus who is inviting them, asking them, to "Take and drink, this is my blood" and yet they refuse.

In a very thoughtful article on the subject of receiving from the chalice, Fr Brian Green of the Hallam Diocese wrote:

> Every time we are at Mass the priest repeats Our Lord's words "take this, all of you, and drink from it". It can be very depressing for the minister of the chalice to be passed by – "sorry I'd rather not drink Christ's blood". It's even more depressing when the local priest has decided there is no option available – "Christ might have wanted it, but I don't".
>
> In the Mass, the separate elements of bread and wine – body and blood – are in fact symbolising the sacrifice which Christ offered in the shedding of his blood. Our emphasis on receiving (only the host) could be making us lose sight of the Mass as a sharing in the Sacrifice of Calvary. There is much to be explored in the symbolism of the cup. In Gethsemane Jesus asked John and James: "are you ready to drink the cup that I am to drink?" Accepting the cup at Mass is itself a potent symbol of our readiness to take up the cross and follow Jesus. What might we be saying when we fail to join in drinking his cup?

Fr Gerald O'Mahony SJ makes the same point in his book *The Mass From Start to Finish*[2] in the section entitled "Communion with Jesus in the chalice". He writes:

> Jesus made the same requirement for the bread and for the wine. He did not say to eat his body but to be very restrictive about his blood. Admittedly, there is an inbuilt restriction of a sort, which is not often referred

> to: Jesus linked the chalice with his suffering. 'Can you drink the chalice that I drink?' asks Jesus of James and John, meaning 'Can you suffer alongside me?' As the presiding priest stands in the central place offering the bread of life to those who come up for it, he is offering them Jesus' unconditional love-unto-death with each host. Then the one presiding invites them, implicitly, to go and receive the chalice, if they are willing to answer with James and John, 'Yes, we will carry the cross beside you.' Not everyone can rise to that, and fair enough. (But) in many cases, the courage comes with the chalice: if we do the action, the understanding and the grace follow. The sign of drinking the Precious Blood is (also) a sign of resurrection, since it reunites the human and divine life of Jesus with his body in the one who drinks his blood.

Perhaps it isn't surprising that some may be reluctant to take what they see as a "new" step especially if the change-in-practice hasn't been explained very well. But, as we have seen, it isn't actually a new practice: Jesus consecrated both bread and wine, inviting his disciples to receive both his body and his blood and that was how the early Church celebrated the Eucharist and that was how the sacrament used to be received. All the Church has done is to restore that ancient practice.

People should have the opportunity (indeed they have the right) to experience the sign of the sacrament more completely by receiving Communion under both kinds and that is the provision that priests are now required to make. At one time we had an excuse for receiving only the body of Christ: that's all that was offered and the theology of the situation is what was taught. The Church has now restored things to how they used to be and has updated its theology and teaching accordingly.

Hopefully, also, when children are being prepared for their First Communion, they are not being taught that receiving from the chalice is an *option*. For their generation it really isn't – just as it should no longer be for ours. It is very easy for children be given a taste of the wine as part of their preparation in order to remove what could be an unnecessary distraction on the day and to make sure that there are no problems with young taste buds! If one or two don't like the taste, then receiving from the chalice can be postponed until they are older and may, by then, have developed a taste for it. Precisely because such concerns can be dealt with ahead of time, they shouldn't become reasons for offering children the option of not receiving from the chalice. It shouldn't be an option unless, as with some adults, they simply don't like the taste. (Receiving the host in the hand should not be an option either – that's how we are now invited to receive. Adult hang-ups about receiving Communion shouldn't be passed on to our children.)

Whilst the graces of the sacrament are not restricted by receiving Communion under one kind only, when Our Lord's invitation was – and still is – "take and eat, this is my body…take and drink, this is my blood", why[3] would we refuse to accept the fullness of that invitation? Yes we have a choice but, especially in this particular context, why would we want one?

NOTES

1 That is, both bread and wine.
2 Kevin Mayhew publications.
3 Unless there are extenuating circumstances.

11

# MEATLESS FRIDAYS

> It would seem that when abstaining from meat went by the board we thought we could forget about Fridays. For forty-five years it has been a particularly well-kept secret that that isn't, in fact, the case.

It's a bit sad, really, when traditions vanish without a trace. Once upon a time a Catholic would never pass a Catholic church without calling in to spend a few minutes in prayer before the Blessed Sacrament – "paying a visit" as we used to say. Nowadays you'd be lucky to find a church open in the first place – another sign of the times – and because that's been the situation for some years now, younger generations of Catholics have never developed the practice. As a result the Blessed Sacrament goes largely unvisited; even if a church is locked, you can still pause and pray as you pass.

Another traditional practice that has gone by the board is that of abstaining from meat on Fridays. If there was one thing that everyone knew about Catholics, it was that they didn't eat meat on Fridays. Sadly younger generations of Catholics these days wouldn't even know that about themselves any more much less do they do it. I say "sadly" not because I'm saddened by the loss of this particular practice, but that we have gradually lost a number of traditions that used to be important to us even if we didn't always fully understand why we did them. If we had understood, perhaps we wouldn't have let them fall by the wayside quite so readily, and not eating meat on Fridays is a case in point.

Why meat and why Fridays? Well, Friday because that was the day on which Our Lord was crucified. By tradition it became associated with acts of penance and spiritual devotions (First Fridays, novenas, devotion to the Sacred Heart, etc.) associated with making reparation for the sins that caused Our Lord to die on the cross for us. And meat because at one time it probably constituted an important part of people's diet and to go without it for an entire day involved a degree of sacrifice and would have left them without a source of nourishment and energy at a time when there was little else available. These days it is no hardship at all to go without meat – not only because there are so many other alternatives, but also because we are so well fed that we are unlikely to miss one item from our diet for a day.

And this is the point really. If not eating meat for one day is no real hardship anymore, then ought we to have found something else to do to mark what should still be a significant day (Friday) for us? Well yes, because, as it turns out, no one actually changed Church teaching on the subject – not even Vatican II as many think. We are still meant to be marking Fridays, but we seem to have conveniently forgotten – a situation that it's difficult to understand given that it was a sin, and confessional matter, to deliberately eat meat on Fridays. If it isn't any more, who said so?

Canon 1251 of the *Code of Canon Law* states:

> Abstinence from meat, or from some other food as determined by the Episcopal Conference, is to be observed on all Fridays, unless a solemnity should fall on a Friday. Abstinence and fasting are to be observed on Ash Wednesday and Good Friday[1]

and that's probably exactly what it has always said. What the Code now goes on to say is that:

> The Episcopal Conference can determine more particular ways in which fasting and abstinence are to be observed. In place of abstinence or fasting it can substitute, in whole or in part, other forms of penance, especially works of charity and exercises of piety (CC.1253).

and that's the bit we seem to have missed post-Vatican II.

It wasn't actually Vatican II that changed things, but an Apostolic Constitution on Penance, *Paenitemini*, issued by

Pope Paul VI in 1966 – the year after the Council ended. In it he announced that new penitential practices ("more suited to our times") would be introduced, but that it would be up to individual bishops' conferences to determine exactly what local practice would be. While, he said, the Church would in general continue to observe the penitential practice of abstaining from meat on Fridays, that could be replaced "with exercises of prayer and works of charity" if that's what the local bishops' conference decided. As a result, the traditional practice in this country of not eating meat on Fridays became a matter of personal choice and it was no longer, therefore, a sin to eat meat.

The one area in which there was to be no choice was with regard to Lent when, the Pope said, the obligation to abstain from meat would apply not only to Ash Wednesday and Good Friday, but to all the Fridays of Lent. However, by the time the document was published, there had been a change of heart and the decision with regard to abstinence was again left to local bishops' conferences which were permitted to substitute abstinence (on days other than Ash Wednesday and Good Friday) "with other forms of penitence and especially works of charity and the exercises of piety" – as our bishops did.

To be honest, while I can definitely remember the general requirement of Friday abstinence being dropped, I can only vaguely remember the rest of the teaching that if we chose not to eat meat Fridays were still to be days of penance observed by practising works of charity or by doing something spiritual, something extra, and that there was no longer any consequence in terms of sin for not doing so (at least that was my impression at the time).

Because we no longer have to think about abstinence (and fasting) other than on just two days of the year (Ash Wednesday and Good Friday) when it is still compulsory, it can be very easy to forget that we are meant to be doing something on Fridays instead. Many people chose to continue abstaining from meat (and it would be a particularly appropriate thing to do during Lent whether officially required or not) because it was easier to remember to do something they had been doing out of habit for years than to have to remember to do something else instead, something that wasn't habitual, something that they would have to think about doing. Those who stopped not eating meat joined the up-and-coming generation who had never not eaten meat in the first place and, forgetting (or never having known) the primary purpose of commemorating Friday as a special day, that association was soon lost as well.

An American commentary[2] on Canon Law that was recommended to us in the seminary, offers some interesting reflections drawn from two (U.S.) National Conference of Catholic Bishops sources.[3]

> Abstinence from meat on all Fridays of the year [while not compulsory] is especially recommended. Also recommended is prayer, penance (especially by eating less food) and almsgiving… for the sake of world peace (and) the reason of self-denial in remembrance of the passion of the Lord as well as "freely and out of love for Christ crucified show(ing) our solidarity with generations of believers to whom this practice frequently became, especially in times of persecution and of great poverty, no mean evidence of fidelity to Christ and His Church."
>
> It is also a continuous reminder of our need of repentance and conversion: "we shall thus also remind ourselves that as Christians, although immersed in the world and sharing its life, we must preserve a saving and necessary difference from the spirit of the world. Our deliberate abstinence from meat, more especially because no longer required by law, will be an outward sign of the spiritual values that we cherish."

And so, how can parents and teachers instil in Catholic youngsters (and priests in Catholic adults) once again the practice *still required by the Church* of making Fridays special because of their association with Our Lord's crucifixion – either by voluntarily abstaining from meat, or by some other act of penance or self-denial, or by some specific spiritual exercise? The fact that, for the last forty-five years, we should never have not been doing something has been a particularly well-kept secret. As soon as the aspect of obligation and sin was removed from the picture, we all-too-easily opted for the easy option of doing nothing (and North Sea cod stocks plummeted anyway!). Meatless Fridays don't have to be a thing of the past, but it seems so much better not only to know what the significance of the practice is, but that we are doing whatever we do by choice and not out of obligation.

## NOTES

1 The law of abstinence applies to all those of fourteen years of age and older (strictly speaking from the day after they are fourteen) The obligation to fast applies to those aged eighteen to fifty-eight inclusive (again strictly speaking from the day after they are eighteen until the day after they are fifty-nine).

2 *The Pastoral Companion* by John M. Huels.

3 One source I was reading said that the NCCB might even be considering rescinding its earlier decision and require American Catholics to abstain from meat on Fridays once again as an expression of their Catholicity and in reparation for the grave sin of abortion.

12

# ASPECTS OF LENT

This article looks at various aspects of the season of Lent and offers some thoughts on better appreciating the meaning of our Lenten practices and symbols.

What got me started on this is what usually gets me started on such things – looking up a word in the dictionary, in this case the word 'Lent'. It turns out (and I don't think I had realised this before) that it comes from Middle/Old English (*lente/lencten*) and Germanic (*lang-*) referring to the lengthening days of spring. The Saxons called March *lenctern monath* because during that month the days noticeably lengthened. So, in that sense, it was initially a seasonal time on the calendar rather than a religious or liturgical time of the year.

That led me to look things up in a number of other sources[1] from which I will borrow heavily in offering the following combination of information which I hope will prove informative. Maybe you already know most of this; maybe you don't – we'll see.

Lent is the name given to the forty-day period of prayer, fasting and penance, between Ash Wednesday and Easter. *The General Instruction of the Roman Missal* says that Lent lasts from Ash Wednesday to the Mass of the Lord's Supper (on Maundy Thursday) exclusive – which means that Ash Wednesday and the three days of the *Easter Triduum* are not actually part of Lent. [My comment: It really doesn't matter exactly how many days there are in Lent and which days they are. The point is to use whatever time there is in the way it is intended: for our personal spiritual growth and as a penitential season in preparation for Easter.]

On Ash Wednesday it is traditional to be signed on the forehead with ashes (obtained from burning the previous year's palms). In various places in the Old Testament, reference is made to wearing sackcloth and being covered with ashes as a public sign of mourning, or as an external sign of sorrow and penance for sin. It is in this regard that the Church has traditionally marked the beginning of the season of Lent with the blessing and distribution of ashes as a sign of our sorrow and repentance for sin.

[A personal comment: Recognising and appreciating the meaning behind the action suggests the inappropriateness of presenting innocent babies and small children to be anointed with ashes. Not only do they not understand what it is they are doing (as an adult would), but, more importantly, what sins do they have to be sorry for? People's response to what I have just said may depend on how well they have understood the symbolism of receiving the ashes. This past Ash Wednesday, three people came to me after Mass to ask for the ashes; they hadn't arrived for Mass in time to receive Communion, but were intent on receiving the ashes. There's almost a superstition involved – that it's Ash Wednesday and therefore we must receive the ashes. What might that be saying about their understanding of what receiving the ashes is all about, especially when Mass and Communion should have been a priority?]

In the first centuries of the Church only two days – Good Friday and Holy Saturday – were observed as days of penance and fasting. This was then extended to the whole of Holy Week, then to the three weeks leading up to Easter, and later still to all six weeks before Easter. One source says that since Sundays were never days of fasting, this amounted to only thirty-six days and so a further four were added to make forty in imitation of Our Lord's fast of forty days in the desert.

[My own comment: The point about Sundays not counting as part of the Lenten fast is something I have heard people claim, but I always took it to be the invention of those who were lookng for an excuse to take even a one-day break from whatever it was they had decided to give up for Lent. If the encyclopaedia is correct then perhaps they were right after all. Indeed it would seem to be backed up by scripture when you stop and think about it. In the "Prayer of the Church" for the Sundays of Lent, the scripture reading for Morning Prayer is taken from the prophet Nehemiah (8:9-10) and reads: *This day is holy to the Lord your God; do not mourn or weep. For this day is holy to our Lord; and do not be grieved, for the joy of the Lord is your strength* – which would seem to suggest that the Sundays of Lent (as with all Sundays) are not meant to be days of fasting, but days of joy and celebration.]

Lent was traditionally divided into two parts: *Quadragesima* (from Ash Wednesday until the Saturday before Passion Sunday) and *Passiontide* (from Passion Sunday until the evening of Holy Saturday.)

[My own comment: Passion Sunday used to be two weeks before Easter and was followed by Palm Sunday, whereas the two Sundays are now combined and celebrated on the last Sunday before Easter. This accounts for why, in the Ordo, there is still an instruction that if it is the custom, crosses and images may be covered from what is now the Fifth Sunday of Lent – two weeks before Easter and a week before Palm Sunday when we enter into the Passion and Holy Week on our modern calendar.]

The Fourth Sunday of Lent was traditionally known as Laetare Sunday – the word laetare ("rejoice") being the first word of the Opening Prayer of the Mass (the Introit, as it was called). The priest used to wear rose-coloured vestments instead of purple (now no longer the practice everywhere) to emphasise the more joyful aspect of the day. In the early Church, the Lenten fast did not begin until the following day and so this Sunday was a joyful celebration before the penitence of Lent began. Later, when the fast was extended, Laetare Sunday was seen as a sort of mid-Lent "relaxation" from our penitential efforts, a "day off" as it were.

The Fourth Sunday also happens to be Mothering Sunday said to derive from the pre-Reformation custom of people visiting their cathedral or mother church on that day; or from the custom of children who were away from home – especially daughters in service – visiting their mothers and families on this day; or from the various references to motherhood in the reading from Galatians (4:22-31) which was the epistle for the day in the old missal.

The original purpose of Lent was as a period of final preparation for catechumens (those receiving instruction in the faith) prior to their baptism at Easter. For everyone else, as a preparation for Easter, it was a time of penance and almsgiving. Public penitents, as was the custom, were excluded from the church from Ash Wednesday until Maundy Thursday. In Rome penitential processions took place daily during Lent, ending each day at the church of a different saint or martyr as part of the eighty-four station days of the year – days of fasting until the end of Mass. (The word station was from the Latin meaning "to stand" – because the days involved walking and standing.)

In the early centuries, observance of the Lenten fast was very rigid: only one meal a day was allowed and meat and fish were both forbidden. In the West the fast was gradually relaxed until it applied only to Ash Wednesday and Good Friday and fish could be eaten.

[These final paragraphs are my own thoughts.]

More recently the law governing these two days of fast and abstinence were relaxed still further. Those of us "of a certain age", as they say, will be familiar with the requirements still current in Canon Law: Fasting means taking only one full meal though some nourishment (restricted in quantity and quality) may also be taken in the morning and evening; eating between meals is not permitted. The law of abstinence forbids the eating of meat but not fish (though meat flavoured soups are permitted).

Our *Diocesan Year Book*, however, contains the current guidelines of our Bishops' Conference (which has authority to make its own interpretations and decisions in this matter). Fasting, it says, means that the amount of food we eat should be considerably reduced (but it doesn't include specific details regarding by how much), and abstinence means that we give up a particular kind of food (without specifying which) or some form of amusement. It all seems a lot more lenient than it used to be and, perhaps, a little confusing. I think, rather than allowing that to be an excuse for doing little or nothing, it invites us to enter into the spirit of what fasting and abstinence are about on these two days in particular, and to make our decisions maturely out of a freedom of choice rather than blind obedience to the letter of the law.

No different decision, however, seems to be have made in terms of who must observe the requirements of fasting and abstaining – and their observance is obligatory. Canon Law says that the law of fasting applies to those aged eighteen to fifty-eight inclusive (strictly speaking from the day after their eighteenth birthday to the day after their fifty-ninth). Abstinence applies to those who have completed their fourteenth year (strictly speaking from the day after their fourteenth birthday). Reasons of ill-health, pregnancy, etc., may excuse of course. Other forms of penance may be chosen by those who are excused or who are not obliged in law.

The Church continues to teach the need to observe Lent as a time of penance, self-denial, and alms-giving, but also for devoting more time than usual to spiritual exercises. This introduces a dimension to Lent that people don't always consider, that of doing something extra (especially spiritually) rather than giving something up. This option shouldn't be embraced simply as an excuse for not practising some degree of self-denial and penance, both of which continue to be important. It should, however, be seen as an opportunity to make Lent a more positive time of personal spiritual growth and development, something which then hopefully becomes a permanent part of our spiritual lives rather than simply being restricted to Lent. It may also help us to welcome Lent rather than dreading its approach!

A final point, and one often overlooked (or, sadly, ignored) is the fact that the Sacrament of Reconciliation (or Confession) is not celebrated during what is called the *Easter Triduum* – the final three days of Holy Week. There are six weeks of Lent in which, appropriately, to celebrate the sacrament of penance. With the celebration of the "Mass of the Lord's Supper" on Maundy Thursday – and its anticipation of the passion and death of Christ – the Church is considered "sacramentally dead" with Christ in the tomb. This is also why we don't celebrate Mass on Good Friday, Communion being offered using hosts (only) consecrated the previous day. No sacraments are celebrated until the Easter Vigil when – in liturgical sign and symbol – we commemorate the fact that Christ is risen.

## NOTE

1 *Virtue's Catholic Encyclopaedia; A-Z of the Catholic Church; Cassell Dictionary of Christianity* and *The Concise Dictionary of the Christian Church.*

13

# *THE PASSAGE OF TIME*

> The pace of society causes us to be constantly planning ahead to the point that we fail to live in, and savour, the present.

I was recently given a newly published book of old photos taken in various towns in Teesside and North Yorkshire at the turn of the nineteenth century, comparing how things used to look then with how they look now. Living in Whitby, I have quite a number of the pictures taken around the town between 1865 and 1910 by local photographer Frank Meadow Sutcliffe and for a while I had equivalent views displayed next to them which I had taken to show how those same views look today.

I really enjoy those sorts of comparative photos; it's just very interesting to see how much some things have changed and, on the other hand, which features have remained pretty much the same despite the passage of time.

You can look, for example, at an Edwardian family group walking along a street and reflect on the fact that in their wildest dreams they couldn't possibly have imagined how that street would look in a hundred years time. They couldn't have imagined for a moment the multi-storey buildings that would one day replace their shops and houses, much less the cars that would be driving along that street at speeds also beyond their imagination. For that matter why would such thoughts have even occurred to them as they quietly strolled along enjoying their Sunday afternoon "constitutional"?

It's the same with us. Can we even begin to imagine how our neighbourhoods and town centres will look a hundred years from now and the changes that might have taken place by then? It's almost impossible really; we simply have no idea, anymore than the Edwardians would have had. Imagination and reality are going to be worlds apart.

Despite all our hopes and plans, even our "dreams", we have no idea what the future holds for us and it becomes an important test of our faith and trust in God that, ultimately, we are content to leave such things entirely in his hands. Only God knows what the future will bring and that should be good enough for us. At the same time it shouldn't stop us from musing and wondering, planning and dreaming, provided we retain a grip on the reality that our only *real* hope lies in God. We don't need to know what the future holds for us – God alone knows – and we leave such things solely in his hands and his providence.

It seems only five minutes since it was Christmas; meanwhile the six weeks of Lent have been and gone, so has Easter, and here we are already thinking about summer holidays! Where on earth does the time go?

They say that time seems to pass more quickly the older you get, but I'm not entirely convinced – and not just because I'm getting older! It seems to me that as you get older, and especially if you don't really want to face the fact, you would try even harder to savour the days as they come and go. Perhaps it's the savouring – making the best use we can of our time and keeping ourselves busy – that makes us less conscious of how time is passing. If we were bored or inactive maybe the days would pass more slowly. It's like when you go on a trip and getting there always seems to take longer than coming back. The anticipation of getting there, looking at everything along the way, seems to make the journey longer than when you are taking less notice, thinking about other things, on the way home.

Perhaps the reason why time seems to pass so quickly is simply that we are so busy – these days more than ever before. We have all sorts of commitments and demands on our time both within our homes and families and outside of them, often finding there just aren't enough hours in the day. Keeping busy and occupied is all very well, but does it come at a price? Are we giving the time we should to others? Are we giving the time we should to God? Do we have any quality time for ourselves, individually or as a family, which is what days off and the Sabbath rest used to be about?

Also, in so many areas of our life, we are constant planning for the future. We move from one event to another, one activity to the next, diaries necessarily to hand. From my own point of view as a priest, I often feel that always having to anticipate and plan for the next church season on the calendar doesn't help the experience that time is flying by, but the danger for me and for all of us in planning constantly for the future is that we can miss out on the present. Today is the tomorrow we planned for yesterday but we never really appreciate it when it arrives because we're already planning for the next tomorrow!

Life can start to feel like we're hanging on to the reins of a runaway horse. The question is: how can we regain control?

In one of his songs, *Secret o' Life*, James Taylor says, "The secret of life is enjoying the passage of time" – not, of course, enjoying its passage but enjoying it as it passes. In other words life isn't just a journey from birth to death, it's about how we spend the time along the way. As Christians, we would have to add that it is also about the purpose of our life, our ultimate goal, eternal life. While our sights are necessarily fixed on the future "as we wait in joyful hope for the coming of our Saviour, Jesus Christ", at the same time that awareness and anticipation should bring our focus very much back to the present because it is in this world, in the here and now, that "we live and move and have our being".

In her book *Death: The Final Stage of Growth*, Elisabeth Kübler-Ross says:

> It is the denial of death that is partially responsible for people living empty purposeless lives, for if you live as if you'll live for ever, it becomes too easy to postpone the things you know you must do. You live your life in preparation for tomorrow or in remembrance of yesterday, and meanwhile each today is lost. In contrast, when you fully understand that each day you awaken could be the last you have, you take time *that day* to grow, to become more of who you really are.

"This is the day the Lord has made, let us rejoice and be glad in it". It's the old adage about taking life one day at a time. *Carpe diem* – "seize the day". The secret of life is enjoying the passage of time – making the most of the here and now. How can we slow down the horses?

> Isn't it a lovely ride, sliding down, gliding down?
> Try not to try too hard. It's just a lovely ride.
>
> (James Taylor, *Secret o' Life*)

14

# A FAMILY DIVIDED

## (Thoughts on Christian Unity)

> This is a reflection on Christian unity, admitting that there continue to be things that, sadly, divide us – issues that are beyond our personal influence other than through our prayers.

Prologue – The Early Days:

For many people, ecumenism (defined as "a movement promoting unity among Christian churches") might seem a relatively recent development. However I recall making an effort in that area back when, as a teenager in the 1960s, I began to attend the local Presbyterian Church youth club. It occurred to me that if I was enjoying the hospitality and facilities of a youth club run by the church my friends attended, then the least I could do, as a courtesy, was to go to a service with them from time to time (it was on a Sunday evening and I'd already been to Mass in the morning so surely that was OK). And so that's what I did – and I didn't get struck by lightning. I say that because the Catholic Church back then taught that you weren't allowed to take part in non-Catholic services, indeed you were barely even allowed inside a non-Catholic church!

I remember that very subject coming up years before when I was in junior school. My Uncle Fred had died and was to have a "Chapel" service and I had asked the headmistress if I was allowed to attend and she said definitely not. When I got home and told my parents that I couldn't go and why not, they said he was my uncle and I was going and that was that. 'Plan B' in such situations was not to join in any of the prayers or hymns – and so I didn't, thus avoiding getting struck by lightning that time too!

The earliest official (and at the time quite innovative) efforts at ecumenical activity that I can remember were as far back as the early 1970s when I was working as a lay-missionary in Zambia. An ecumenical bible study group was organised in the local United Reformed Church hall – I remember we studied St Paul's Letter to the Ephesians – and it was quite an eye-opener to discover (in this case in our approach to the interpretation of scripture) how much we all had in common as opposed to how different we thought we were.

In an episode of the television documentary series "A Seaside Parish", the Anglican vicar featured in the programme was visiting a young couple who had recently had a baby. Responding to the vicar's question about the possibility of a christening, the baby's mother said, "I'm actually a Catholic… but it doesn't really matter." It was almost as if she was apologising for her Catholic upbringing and, at the same time, trying to minimise any embarrassment that might have been caused. Either way, it struck me as a rather sad thing for someone to say. I also know of a situation where, in order to demonstrate their objection to their parish having been amalgamated, some people go to the Anglican church on those Sundays when there isn't a Mass scheduled in their former parish church, claiming "it's all the same"!

In our ecumenical relationships and our hopes of once again uniting our divided Christian family, I don't think we can pretend our differences don't exist. In fact I think we have to admit to them and respect them. If they were of no consequence then, presumably, we wouldn't be worshipping God in all the various different ways that we do. The reality – and the sadness – is, however, that our Christian family is divided; it's not how God intended it to be but nonetheless it's the situation we have created. It would be wonderful if there was a magic button we could press that would wipe out the last four hundred and seventy years of our churches' history, but it isn't quite that simple.

On the positive side, with one or two sad exceptions we do seem to have overcome much of the bigotry that once kept us firmly apart, a bigotry that stemmed from our mutual ignorance of one another's spirituality, theology and practices, and a closed-mindedness that excluded any desire better to understand one another. But unfortunately the differences between us are less easily resolved than they were created in the first place.

I don't know if you have ever visited any of the French or Belgian battlefields of the First World War. In most places time has long ago healed the land and, as you look across rich green fields, it's almost impossible to imagine the carnage that once took place there or the resulting devastation. From time to time a farmer will unearth a remnant of barbed wire or an unexploded shell as he ploughs his fields. Elsewhere the remains of trenches are still to be seen, or have actually been preserved for posterity, a monument to the fighting that once took place and a physical reminder that it is something we must never repeat – though, sadly, we have and we do.

We are only too well aware of our church histories and the things that drove us apart, but more often than not we can meet together in the green fields of our common areas of belief – praying together, studying together, celebrating the things we hold in common. At the same time there are still a few trenches, once at the frontline of the conflicts that divided us, aspects of teaching and practice that will continue to keep us apart until greater minds than ours can settle on and decide our common ground and hopefully reunite our Christian family. In the meantime we don't need to be apologetic, rather we need to admit to and accept our differences – otherwise how do we know what areas need to be resolved in order to bring us back together?

In that sense our differences do matter and what makes us good Catholics will make us good Christians. Therefore we need to ask ourselves: What does it mean to be a Catholic? What does my baptism into the Catholic Church require of me? Am I fulfilling not only those requirements, but also all the other duties that I have towards my faith community? And from where do I draw the strength that sustains me in those efforts?

If we don't have conviction in, and a commitment to, the Church to which we belong, the faith community that sustains us, where is our credibility in the eyes of those with whom we hope one day to be reunited? Will we treat belonging with them as lightly as we seem to treat belonging to our current faith family? On a more banal level, it would be rather like what we see with a football player who joins a particular club, is paraded in front of the media in the club's colours, and who states unequivocally his loyalty to his new team as he signs his four-year contract and kisses the club badge on his shirt. Twelve months later, another club puts in a bid and he's off – his contract means nothing – and there he is in front of the media once again, in another set of colours, declaring his loyalty to yet another team as he now signs his name on their dotted line.

It ought to make a difference to us which "dotted line" we signed on at our baptism. It ought to make a difference to us which faith community sustains us spiritually, pastorally and sacramentally. Our Lord's own teaching and that of the Church[1], is that his kingdom is open to all who come to him in faith and even to those who, through no fault of their own, haven't had the word of God preached to them. Even those who claim to be Christian may be making their faith journey unnecessarily difficult, although (as the parable of the wedding garment teaches) none of us can ever afford to become complacent or presumptuous.

Let's say someone were to ask you the best way to go by car to somewhere at the other end of the country. Do you recommend the most scenic route, or the most direct, or the least congested, or the fastest, or simply the one you prefer explaining all the reasons why you prefer it? Surely when it comes to our following of Christ, we have chosen what we consider to be the best way and therefore we not only take that road with conviction and commitment, but we would want to see others discover that same route for themselves, share our experience, and reach the same destination with us, safe and sound.

In his poem "The Elephant in the Room", Terry Kettering writes:

*There's an elephant in the room.*
*It is large and squatting, so it is hard to get around it.*
*Yet we squeeze by with "How are you?" and "I'm fine"*
*and a thousand other forms of trivial chatter.*
*We talk about the weather. We talk about work.*
*We talk about everything else, except the elephant in*
*the room.*

The expression an "elephant in the room" refers to a situation that is glaringly obvious and yet everyone is trying to ignore it as if it doesn't exist because, perhaps, no one knows what to do about it. Christian unity will never be achieved by tip-toeing around the "elephant" of the issues that keep our faith family divided, but can only be helped by an honest admission that we'd like to put the pieces back together again – which necessarily means admitting that differences do indeed exist. And those differences matter because they also help us to recognise our common ground, and it is that which provides a starting point for our hopes and a subject for our prayers.

NOTES

1 John 10:16, and the *Catechism of the Catholic Church*, paras 836-848.

15

# IF ONLY WE HAD KNOWN BETTER

This article addresses the sensitive and difficult issue of child abuse by priests.

As accusations of sexual abuse by priests continue to surface, I'm sure Catholics are looking for reassurance that the Church and the priesthood aren't crumbling around them and that things are not as desperate as the picture popularly painted by the media.

There is no question whatsoever of the basic moral evil underlying all instances of the sexual abuse of children. It is a misuse of power and a betrayal of trust on the part of the abuser and it can result in tremendous long-term psychological harm and damage to the victim. There are no excuses, no mitigating circumstances. Children should be, and must be, completely safe and totally protected, and those who abuse children must be held fully accountable in law. I make these points right at the start because I don't want anyone to misinterpret what I am going to say, or to think that I am in any way lessening the extreme seriousness of the situation of child abuse, in particular on the part of priests.

I had been looking once again at two books that I had read on the subject of child sexual abuse, books that were considered expert presentations on the subject and that were published as recently as the early 1990s. Both of them went in the bin shortly after I re-read parts of them. I couldn't believe how out-dated they had become in so short a space of time and how wrong they now were in some of the recommendations they made at the time. For me this confirms just how ignorant we were as a society on the subject of paedophilia and how much we have learned and how much our approach has had to change in just the last few years.

Much of what we have been hearing in the media recently has had to do with the mismanagement of priests suspected of sexual activity with children. By and large the abuse itself occurred many years ago at a time when the subject of paedophilia was little understood. It was treated in much the same way as priests were dealt with who had a drink problem. At least with alcoholism a priest could be sent to AA for help and he would typically also be moved to a new parish with the hope of new beginnings all round, the priority being to protect the reputation of the priest, to avoid any more scandal than had already been given, and to safeguard the image of the priesthood. Like everyone else at the time, bishops simply had no idea about the pathology of paedophilia or that, like alcoholism, it is an illness – in this case a mental illness – that isn't going to go away and that can't be cured. Moving a priest to another parish was not the answer, nor was it realistic to expect an abusing priest to stay away from children simply by sending him somewhere where children weren't immediately accessible. We now know better, but at the time we didn't and as a result we are now hearing more and more about the mismanagement of priests suspected of abusing children.

If accusations of abuse were made against a priest and those accusations were found to be true, legal process should have followed and the child(ren) involved given appropriate help and support. In practice, cases of abuse weren't easy to prove because victims were afraid to tell anyone, especially when it involved their priest. Initially there would probably have been a degree of secrecy to overcome because the child would have been too afraid to say anything or maybe didn't realise that what was happening to them was wrong because they trusted the priest. Anyone who may have had their suspicions would typically have come up with other explanations first, giving the priest the benefit of the doubt, because the reality was too shocking to contemplate. Only, perhaps, after a considerable amount of time had passed would it have been impossible to continue denying the situation and something would finally have been said.

We can't for a moment deny, or ignore, the effects that past abuse has had on someone as a child, and their needs must now be acknowledged and addressed. But some of the accusations that have been levelled at Church leaders and religious orders have to be seen within the context of what was known at the time. No one can excuse the judgment and action of someone who should have known better, but by the same token we can't look back with hindsight and condemn someone for not acting according to knowledge they simply wouldn't have had at the time – and through no fault of their own.

But this leads to my next point: why has it taken so long for the current wave of cases to come to light?

I understand and accept the psychological damage and trauma that the experience of sexual abuse can cause and, therefore, how difficult it might be for someone to now bring out into the open past experiences they may have been repressing, or even denying, for so many years. Many of the cases currently coming to light seem to have happened in the 1970s and yet, while some made their abuse known let's say ten or fifteen years ago, others have only been able to come forward more recently – which, of course, is quite understandable. However, one obvious consequence of this is that there seems to be no end to the revelations – they just keep coming, one after another. As a result the damage being caused to the Church and to the priesthood by what is actually a very small proportion of priests and religious is far greater than such a minority ought to be able to cause. It's almost like the after-shocks of an earthquake which often cause far more damage than the initial quake did.

We had the scandal of priest-abusers here in England, but then, eventually, things settled down and we hoped we could move on. But then cases came to light in a number of American dioceses and while the far-reaching effects of those scandals have yet to be resolved, things at least began to settle down. But then it was England once again, then Ireland, then Germany, then Italy. It seems like every time things begin to settle and people start getting over their outrage, and the priesthood begins to emerge from the shadow that each case casts, along comes another wave and another and so it goes on. You can't help wondering who or what is behind so well "coordinated" a process. I am quite convinced that it proves the devil is alive and well and is well-served by this situation.

Even when there is a case to be answered by individuals within a local Church, the situation is doing untold and (in terms of the larger picture) undeserved damage to the wider Church. Yes, the Church has to be accountable for what has been going on, but, as I have said, the past actions of what is, again, a small minority of priests should never be able to cause so much potential damage.

In light of how long ago some of the cases of abuse took place, the question has been raised as to whether there should be a "statute of limitations".

First of all there are grounds for concern regarding the reliability of memory with the passage of time. It could be argued that the trauma resulting from abuse may have etched that experience into the memory but, by the same token, if someone has actively repressed the experience over the years, how reliable is whatever remains of those memories? There is also the possibility of false memories created by the imagination or resulting from what a person may have heard or read. The more time that passes, the more risk there is that such factors could have an influence. These things are not easily proved or disproved and what would help is for accusations to be made as soon as possible after the event, while the memories are more immediate and therefore more reliable. That might be possible in an ideal world, but if it were an ideal world there wouldn't have been any abuse in the first place.

Secondly, given that it has taken some victims of abuse twenty or thirty years to come forward, the situation isn't helped by a recent newspaper report which stated that one victim "only complained about the abuse after hearing that another victim had won compensation". Sadly it's our pervading compensation culture that causes people to wonder. At first it seemed that victims were satisfied simply to see the perpetrators of abuse brought to book and therefore also preventing others from being abused. But more recent cases seem to have multi-million pound (or dollar) compensation claims attached to them and, typically, dioceses are not in a financial position to survive such claims. And whether they are or whether they aren't, ultimately it will be the people of those dioceses (not the abusers) who, directly or indirectly, will have to bear the financial cost of the claims being made.

Another time-related concern has to do with accusations of physical, as opposed to sexual, abuse.

The way in which children are disciplined has changed considerably in recent years, in fact there seems to be very little discipline at all any more and maybe that accounts for some of problems we see and experience in our society. Even though the ways in which children used to be disciplined (especially in institutions – and Borstal would be a prime example) would not be acceptable today, it seems unjust and unfair for people to be able bring prosecutions now on the basis of how they were treated twenty or thirty years ago at a time when physical chastisement and discipline were widely accepted and applied in society. Where such acts were excessive and truly abusive, however, then individuals should, of course, be held accountable.

As far as the grim picture of the clergy currently being given is concerned, it has to be said that, statistically, the incidence of abuse by priests is no higher than in the rest of the population – a fact that doesn't seem to be as newsworthy. The point is sadly illustrated by recent high profile cases of the physical and sexual abuse of children by family members, something we find particularly disturbing. Interestingly people wouldn't criticise the institution of the family despite whatever abuse might occur within its walls, but certain elements (including the media) will seize on abuse by priests to criticise the institution of the Church and the priesthood. They will demand the heads of bishops and cardinals, but who do they hold responsible for abuse within families?

What should be said is that people have a right to expect better of their priests, a higher moral standard, and that the trust they place in their clergy should be well-founded. In the vast majority of cases – and that is the important point to remember – this will be so, even though priests are only human and have faults and shortcomings just like everyone else. That said, sexual abuse is something that can, and will, no longer be covered up or excused. If we had known better we would surely have done better and now that we do, we will.

At the same time the priesthood doesn't deserve to be under the constant attack it is currently under as a result of the, albeit horrendous, actions of a minority. From a personal point of view it makes me very angry that they have caused (and continue to cause) so many problems for the rest of us who are simply trying to get on with our ministry. I know of colleagues who have been called (not accused, but called) child abusers simply because they are priests. Why should we have to keep defending and justifying ourselves and our ministry all because of a few bad apples?

Unfortunately priests are now at a point of paranoia in our contact with children (even my use of the word "contact" could be misunderstood – that's how paranoid we have become). We are advised to avoid even the most harmless physical contact with children; we are wary of being alone in a sacristy with an altar server; and we must constantly second-guess every situation we are in that involves children. From a pastoral point of view, none of this helps a child to experience their priest as being friendly and welcoming but, unfortunately, that's how things have to be these days. We are even required to ensure our confessional doors are fitted with a window so we don't create a situation of compromise or risk for the penitent (child or adult) or for ourselves.

There is very little the Church can do to make up for incidents of abuse in the past or for its failure to deal with abusers the way they should have been dealt with had we have known better. However the Church can ensure that if an abuser still in post is discovered, they are immediately and unconditionally removed from their ministry and held to account in law for their actions. Hopefully adequate systems are now in place (in our seminaries and afterwards) to safeguard children and vulnerable adults against physical or sexual abuse – by anyone involved in the Church, not just priests – and to indentify the first signs of deviant behaviour on the part of individuals who, despite everything, may still have managed to slip through the safeguarding net. All that even CRB clearance says is that a possible problem hasn't been discovered yet, therefore because there is never a one hundred percent guarantee, there must never be less than one hundred per cent vigilance.

While the tragic reality of child abuse by clergy cannot be ignored, I think it's important to have a balanced perspective with respect to the vast majority of priests who are doing everything that their people expect of them spiritually and pastorally and in no way deserve to be tarred with the same brush as those found guilty of abuse. However, as long as new cases continue to surface (and many are actually old cases from a time when we didn't know what we know now), it is difficult for priests not to feel that we and our ministry continue to be under a microscope. One way or another it puts that much more pressure on our ministry in an age when there is pressure enough already. And of course, in such a climate, sadly there is little wonder that young people, seeing what they see in the media about priesthood, and not always hearing a voice in support of it, decide that it's no way of life for them. I will always remember the occasion when, at the end of a diocesan celebration at the Cathedral in Middlesbrough, the late Bishop O'Brien spontaneously spoke in support of the priests of the diocese. His words, and the priests who were present, received a very moving and prolonged ovation from a packed congregation. It was just what we needed at the time and it's probably just what we need again now.

16

# ON A MORE POSITIVE NOTE

This article seeks to provide a more positive picture of priesthood and the ministry of priests than the one currently being painted by the media.

In 2005 the total number of Catholic priests throughout the world was just over 400,000. In 2009 there were almost 5000 priests in England & Wales (3,506 diocesan and 1312 religious). The proportion of those guilty of sexually abusing children is extremely small by comparison. That doesn't for a moment lessen the seriousness of what has happened, but it does offer a much more positive picture of priesthood than the one currently being painted by a media always hungry for scandal and any opportunity, it would seem, to criticise the Church.

As I have said before, from a personal point of view, it makes me very angry that a few bad apples have caused, and continue to cause, so many problems for the rest of us, the vast majority of priests, who are simply trying to get on with our ministry. We are all being tarred with the same brush and that is both unjust and unacceptable. No one seems to be speaking up in defence of priests; no one is countering the bad news with good; no one is offering a positive point of view, so I'm going to because I think it's long overdue and much needed.

Firstly, therefore, what is involved in someone becoming a priest?

Initially a candidate for priesthood will have experienced, in a way that is unique to each individual, a calling to be a priest. However long it takes him to recognise and respond to that experience, he will eventually meet with the vocations director for his diocese (or a similar individual if he is considering a religious order) and will be guided through an initial process of discernment, psychological testing, and interviews with a vocations panel and others. If all indicators are positive, he will then meet with his bishop to discuss admission to a seminary to begin formal training which may also include studying for a degree (younger candidates may be required to spend a pre-seminary year of preparation and study first). Training for the priesthood usually takes six years, studying subjects such as theology, philosophy, Church history, moral theology, Canon Law and liturgy, and students will be given practical pastoral experience by working in parishes, hospitals, schools, prisons, and so on. They also receive regular spiritual direction as well as making an annual retreat. Introduction into increasing levels of ministry along the way will eventually lead to their vowed commitment to celibacy and to ordination as a deacon and then as a priest, by which time Church Law requires they be at least twenty-five years of age.

So often in parishes it is typically a bit of an uphill battle to get people to take part in preparation programmes prior to the celebration of the sacraments even though such programmes may be only a matter of weeks or perhaps even days, and yet people wouldn't object for a moment to candidates for the priesthood having to spend six years in the seminary prior to priestly ordination. But that's what it involves – six years of full time study, training, preparation, and testing of their vocation – and, really, should it involve anything less given the importance of the ministry they will eventually be ordained to carry out?

Secondly, then, what is that ministry all about? What might a priest's typical day and week look like? (And I would like to dispel at this point the popular myth that a priest works only on Sundays!)

Much will depend on the parish a priest is in, because every parish is different and the things he will be called upon to do will therefore also be different. There are the obvious things such as celebrating Mass each day, hearing confessions (usually once a week), and celebrating baptisms, the occasional wedding and (usually far from occasional) funerals. There may be a parish school to visit from time to time; a hospital of which he may be the chaplain; nursing homes to visit; and possibly a prison.

Parish visiting in the way it used to be done when there were often several priests in a parish is largely no longer possible simply because of the time constraints that most parish priests now experience as a result of being on their own in a parish and having to be a "parish manager" rather than simply a parish priest. Thankfully lay people have, in recent years, taken up once again ministries that complement that of the priest so that pastoral needs are served and the priest doesn't need to be running round like the proverbial headless chicken trying to do everything himself!

The following could be a typical day for a priest. He gets up, has some breakfast, says his Office, and then celebrates morning Mass. He deals with the day's post (if it comes that early!) and, after a quick trip to the supermarket, heads out to visit a bereaved family to discuss the funeral with them. On the way back he calls in to the parish school and manages to visit most of the classes to say hello and to see what they are doing. Back home he grabs a bite to eat before a 1pm appointment with a building contractor who is coming to look at a rising damp problem in the church hall. The contractor is half an hour late and so the priest only just makes it in time to the deanery meeting in the neighbouring parish. Late afternoon, back home, he has several phone calls to return and, with no secretary, bills to pay. He manages to put his feet up for twenty minutes while he watches the news headlines. He cooks and eats his dinner rather hurriedly because he has a couple coming to see him about a wedding. They too are late making him, in turn, late for the Parish Council meeting at seven which goes on much longer than expected and so he doesn't get to finally say his Office and put his feet up until after nine o'clock. Half way through a programme he has been waiting all week to watch the phone rings and he is off to the hospital to anoint someone who is dying and by the time he gets back home it has been a fifteen hour day.

Everyone assumes that the things a priest may be called on to do are easy for him and so his ministry in those areas is often be taken for granted. Priests are just like everyone else with their strengths and weaknesses, abilities and limitations. Ordination isn't a cure-all.

Not everyone enjoys going into hospitals to visit and may have a real problem with the hospital setting. Priests are no different and yet they have to go because it's part of what they do and it's what people expect of them. Or, for example, how comfortable would you be in the presence of, or having to touch, a dead body? Regardless of how he feels, a priest is expected to pray with families in the presence of someone who has died, signing the body with the Sign of the Cross. And one of the more difficult things that a priest has to do is to be with families who have been bereaved. It is extremely difficult suddenly to have to step into a family's grief and try to provide sensitively both ministry and support to them in their needs. (Ten minutes later he could be at a celebratory gathering in school for a teacher who is retiring and, within the hour, have to step back into a situation of grief with another bereaved family.) But it's what is expected of a priest, it's what he does – often several times a week but no less personally on each occasion. But there is never a front page headline: "Catholic priest comforts grieving families".

It goes without saying that one of the most important things a priest does is to celebrate the Eucharist. Without the priest there can be no Eucharist. Consider, also, the healing that he helps people to experience by celebrating the sacrament of reconciliation with them. Only a priest can do that. And just think of all the baptisms he celebrates and the weddings he conducts and, for a bishop, all the confirmations and the ordinations of the next generation of priests. None of that makes the headlines either: "Priest celebrates Mass for 300", "Catholic priest brings inner healing through Confession", "Families line up for baptism by priest"!

Hopefully when someone has a problem they need to talk about, rather than spending a fortune on a counsellor they remember their priest. No priest is an expert on everything (if only!), nor will he necessarily have the greatest counselling skills, but as a priest he brings something to the situation that other professionals can't simply by virtue of his priesthood. How many marriages have priests helped to save? How many suicides have they helped prevent? How many alcoholics have they helped turn their lives around? That won't make the front pages either.

Throughout the world there are thousands of missionary priests helping to spread the gospel and bring people to faith and salvation through the sacraments of the Church, often in conditions that most people wouldn't tolerate for a week let alone a lifetime. Where are the headlines? And there are priests being held in prisons throughout the world, simply for having borne witness on behalf of their people to situations of injustice and corruption. Why isn't the media telling their story?

Of course most of the things I have mentioned are simply part of a priest's ministry; it's what he does; there is no reason for headlines. But unfortunately when priests do make the news for the wrong reasons, that's all that people hear. There is no good news to help redress the balance, no "but on the other hand..." stories. The vast majority of priests are good men – not perfect, but generally good – who, day in day out, quietly get on with their ministry, serving their people and trying to live up to their expectations (never an easy task!). Not for a moment to deny the seriousness of what abusing priests have done, but why is it that this has become all that the priesthood is about at the moment? The media are making it possible for the actions of a sad and sick minority who have already caused enough damage to the lives of the victims of their abuse, to now cause even more damage – this time to the priesthood and the Church.

Never wanting to spoil a good story, the media also seems conveniently to forget to mention that the incidence of abuse by priests is no more than in the general population. There have always been "bogey men" and "dirty old men" in mackintoshes; children have always suffered abuse at the hands of fathers, uncles (and "uncles") and even mothers and others, but the witch hunt doesn't seem to turn its attention to those areas of our society. As trustworthy as priests should be, surely a child's own parents should be even more so. Why, then, is all the media focus only on priests?

As long as this continues, we find ourselves having to minister under a cloud of suspicion that we don't deserve.

One way or another it puts that much more pressure on our ministry in an age when there is pressure enough already. And of course, in such a climate, sadly there is little wonder that young people, seeing what they see in the media about priesthood and not always hearing a voice in support of it, decide that it's no way of life for them. Ultimately the people of our parishes will suffer as the number of priests available to serve them declines. Prayer is our ultimate hope: prayer for a priesthood currently under siege[1] and prayer for vocations in spite of it.

NOTES

1 (and specifically for our bishops and our Holy Father)

17

# HONESTLY?

A reflection on truth and honesty and the potential ill-effects of what can become almost casual lying. Also the issue of trust and keeping confidences.

*"The eighth commandment forbids misrepresenting the truth in our relations with others. This moral prescription flows from (our) vocation to bear witness to (our) God who is the truth and wills the truth."*[1]

## What colour is the truth?

People will sometimes confess to telling a "white lie", however lies don't really come in colours! The phrase "white lie" does appear in the dictionary and is defined as "a diplomatic or well-intentioned untruth", but a lie is a lie no matter how diplomatic or well-intentioned. Politicians will often accuse one another of being "economical with the truth" which doesn't imply that they have lied but that they haven't necessarily told the whole truth – which is still dishonest and perhaps even deceitful.

Even though it may be fictional, we see so often in television plays and films that lies trip so easily off characters' tongues – more easily than the truth a lot of the time – which serves only to portray casual lying as being the norm. The catechism says that "the *gravity* of a lie is measured against the nature of the truth it deforms, the circumstances involved, the intention of the one who lies, and the harm suffered by its victims" (para. 2484). However no lie is ever excusable: "Lying is the most direct offence against the truth… by its very nature, (it) is to be condemned" (para's 2483/86).

At its most basic level, just like swearing and using bad language, telling lies is an abuse of the gift of speech. More than that, however, it also involves something we don't always consider and that is how lying affects other people, possibly even putting them at risk, leading them astray, deceived by the lies we have told. People sometimes use the word "fib", which the dictionary defines as "an inconsequential lie" as if there are no consequences to telling lies. I'm sure we've all experienced being lied to and so we all know what that feels like. Sometimes it can be over something quite trivial in which case it probably causes us nothing more than a feeling of disappointment toward the person who told the lie. On the other hand the experience of being deliberately deceived, being taken advantage of and having our trust abused, can have very negative and long-lasting consequences.

The catechism refers to such consequences (or at least the lying that caused them) as an offence against justice and charity. Most priests regularly experience such "offences against charity" on the part of the very people who come asking *for* charity. The stories of those knocking on presbytery doors looking for hand-outs are legendary, every possible heartstring-tugging, hard luck story you can imagine, we have heard them all. Sadly experience shows that, unlike in the days when such callers were genuinely in need (what we used to refer to as "tramps" or, more politely, "gentlemen of the road"), these days most are con artists to the point that in some places the various church leaders have found it necessary to introduce a system of alerting one another by phone to callers doing the rounds.[2]

As I try to say to people in confession, to be known as someone who can be trusted with the truth is a very precious quality and, once lost, it can be very difficult to regain. If, sadly, we have given grounds for people to think we can't be trusted with the truth or to tell the truth, how can we persuade people to the contrary? – our efforts at persuasion may themselves not be trustworthy. We can probably only persuade by the example we then set and this can take a long time. Better to safeguard the quality in the first place.

In many cases telling a lie is probably a defensive reaction that happens before we can stop ourselves – which is a possible explanation, but not an excuse. We tell a lie in order to avoid the consequence of something we have done that was wrong, but now we have done two things wrong – the original action and then the lie to cover it up. The obvious, though possibly less pleasant, option is to tell the truth and accept the consequences of what we did, but that may take decision-making and some degree of courage and the lie can slip out more easily – again an explanation, not an excuse.

There may be situations in which we may feel it is justified to tell a "white lie", for example to protect someone, a "well-intentioned untruth" as the dictionary puts it. But then we have to remember that no lie is ever justified and we should bear this in mind one or two stages earlier in our decision-making so as not to put ourselves in a situation where a lie results. The catechism cautions us that, in a given situation, "we must judge whether or not it is appropriate to reveal the truth to someone who asks for it"(para. 2488). But this means discerning the situation before we get into it. "The good and safety of others, respect for privacy, and the common good are sufficient reasons for being silent about what ought not to be known… No one is bound to reveal the truth to someone who does not have the right [or, we might say, the need] to know it" (para. 2489). Silence may be our only option, rather than telling a lie.

One of the things we must also think about is gossiping. The basic problem with gossip is that it usually involves talking about another person in their absence and, apart from being uncharitable, it may also involve what the catechism calls either "detraction" or "calumny".[3] A person is guilty of detraction "who without objectively valid reason, discloses another's faults and failings to persons who did not know them", or of calumny "who, by remarks contrary to the truth, harms the reputation of others and gives occasion for false judgments concerning them" (para. 2477). The latter is easily put right because, as it says, calumny involves telling an untruth about someone and so we can hopefully persuade everyone whom we told that what we said was a lie.[4] However we can never undo the harm we cause to someone by detraction given that what we said of the person was the truth. If we said we had lied, that in itself would be a lie. "Detraction and calumny destroy the reputation and honour of one's neighbour and everyone enjoys a natural right to the honour of his/her name and reputation and to respect" (para. 2479) – no matter what we may know to be true about them.

## Whatever happened to integrity (not to mention trust and confidentiality)?

It was Francis Bacon (1561-1626) who said that knowledge is power. The purpose of the childhood taunt: "I know a secret, I know a secret!", was to instil both jealousy and curiosity until we let the other person in on the secret. Some people are good at keeping secrets (to this day my mother won't talk about what she did during the Second World War because she signed the Official Secrets Act at the time). Others are absolutely hopeless at keeping something to themselves that they have been told "in confidence". The fact that they know something that others don't eats away at them until they leak like a sieve.

The word "confidence" means that something is shared "in great trust" (*com-fidere*) – that something private is entrusted to another – and it's that aspect of trust that is important. We know only too well from everyday examples involving butlers or housekeepers or private secretaries to the rich and famous that people can't always be trusted to keep confidences or to respect another's right to privacy. Media money talks and so do they. There is nothing, in fact, to stop them talking except the basic principles of trust and confidentiality, but neither one seems to mean anything any more.

It's one of the reasons why it can be difficult for people to accept – and trust – the *seal of confession*: that a priest is forbidden to reveal anything to anyone under any circumstance whatsoever that he has heard within the context of the sacrament. The fact that he is forbidden under threat of excommunication doesn't seem to help people's sense of trust in that most sacred of confidences. They think that most people can't keep a secret – or, perhaps, they know that they can't – and therefore they don't accept that a priest can and will… and yet he does. Before God he has to.

In the normal circumstances of everyday life, experience seems to show that there isn't a lot of integrity around these days. Defined as "strict adherence to a code of moral values or other standards; complete sincerity or honesty", it's the glue of integrity that holds so many facets of our society together.

There isn't actually anything – nothing physical that is – to stop us from acting in a way that lacks integrity. Integrity is governed by internal principles and it is the strength of those principles, and the degree to which they are governed by honesty and trust, that will influence our actions. If someone tells us a secret or tells us something in strict confidence[5], how do we handle that knowledge? Does knowledge become power? Does the fact that we know something that someone else doesn't become too much for us to handle, or do we have sufficient principle and self-discipline to maintain the confidentiality and so justify the trust that has been placed in us? If we can't, then it's dishonest of us to pretend otherwise.

Everything comes back to honesty and whether we can be trusted – whether with the truth or with anything else. "It is in accordance with their dignity that all people are both impelled by their nature and bound by a moral obligation to seek the truth, especially religious truth. They are also bound to adhere to the truth once they come to know it and direct their whole lives in accordance with the demands of truth." [6]

Honestly? Yes, honestly.

NOTES

1 *Catechism of the Catholic Church* (Chapman 1994), para. 2464.
2 All they want is money, usually for drugs or drink. You can offer to buy them food at the supermarket or to buy them a bus ticket to the family funeral they've told you about, but they will refuse. What they want is cash in hand for drink or drugs or whatever, and they will tell whatever story they have to, to con that out of you.
3 Both of these are discussed as offences against the truth and the eighth commandment – bearing false witness against our neighbour.
4 Something we are obliged to do in conscience. Every offence committed against justice and truth entails the duty of reparation (para. 2487).
5 And it is never an excuse to pass on that knowledge to someone else "in strictest confidence".
6 para. 2467 of the catechism.

18

# PUTTING CHRIST BACK INTO CHRISTMAS

> My annual attempt to try to get people to focus on the true meaning of Christmas and to resist the premature excesses of the High Street.

## Advent: A Time of *Waiting*

In the midst of all the typical pre-Christmas mayhem which, try as we might, we won't be able to avoid, Advent provides us with a few weeks grace to put the genie back in the bottle, the credit card back in the wallet, and to step back from the brink and think. It also calls us to a time of very necessary spiritual preparation in order to remind ourselves that, as Christians, *we* don't celebrate the birth until the baby is born.

The word Advent comes from the Latin *advenire*, meaning "to come to". As our Advent wreath and calendar[1] are designed to remind us, step by step we move from the darkness of anticipation toward the light of revelation. If the event is worth waiting for, then let's wait. It's bad enough that the High Street has been doing its version of Christmas possibly since as early as September, and that some of our neighbours' houses will be decorated weeks ahead of Christmas. But this is *our* feast and it doesn't begin until December 25th and it continues until the Epiphany, don't forget, so don't be fooled by those who start taking down their decorations the minute they get back from the pub on Boxing Day!

We have four weeks of Advent in which to prepare for the coming of Christ. It's our feast and we should prepare for it in our own way – not the Christmas shopping, not writing cards, not baking cakes (though we may have all of that to do as well), but very deliberately making the spiritual journey from darkness to light, taking the time and making the time for that journey, counting down the days and making them count – spiritually. That's the invitation from the church when we begin our Advent season.

It's one of the reasons why I personally won't get involved in Christmas carol services. By definition Christmas carols are songs of praise and joy celebrating the birth of Christ. On two counts, therefore, we shouldn't be singing them before Christmas: firstly because the Church teaches that Advent is a penitential season, not one of praise and joy, hence purple vestments are worn throughout, and, secondly, because Christ isn't born yet and so Christmas carols are totally inappropriate during Advent.

If we join the world around us in celebrating aspects of Christmas while it's still only Advent, then we lose the whole spiritual purpose of the season and by the time our proper celebrations begin on Christmas Day we can already be suffering from "Christmas fatigue". We can't afford to allow our celebration to be compromised by what everyone else considers Christmas to be all about, or, to put it another way, if we don't fight our spiritual corner, then who is going to? We don't celebrate the birth until the baby is born.

We simply need to be patient and disciplined. It's not as if, if we don't jump on the bandwagon, we're going to miss anything. Christmas, the *real* Christmas, won't start without us and *our* journey getting there must first include Advent – a time of waiting, a time of anticipation.

## Reclaiming the Feast

How we "traditionally" celebrate Christmas, in the non-spiritual sense, is actually a very short tradition with many of the things we associate with Christmas being either pagan in origin[2] or the fruit of a Victorian idealised Christmas that embraced certain traditional elements as well as others that were developments of their own time.

It was Prince Albert, for example, who in 1841 first introduced the German custom of the Christmas tree to this country.[3] The first Christmas card wasn't produced until 1843. And it was the Victorians who revived the medieval custom of carolling.

The origins of Santa Claus can be traced to the gift-giving fourth-century bishop from modern-day Turkey,

St Nicholas, patron saint of children and seafarers (feast day 6 December). In Holland he was known as "Sinter Klaas" and became associated with gift-giving at Christmas, a tradition and image that Dutch immigrants then took to the United States where the name Santa Claus developed. It was an 1823 illustration of the Santa Claus figure in the poem *The Night Before Christmas* that has become our traditional image.[4] In 1843, Charles Dickens wrote *A Christmas Carol*, a book that immortalised the Victorian Christmas – including the jolly, larger-than-life Dickensian "Spirit of Christmas Present" we call Father Christmas. One source[5] suggests that most images prior to about 1880 showed Fr Christmas with a green coat and that red only became popular after Coca-Cola introduced it in their advertisements in America in the 1930s.[6]

If, therefore, so much of our so-called traditional Christmas is only around 170 years old, how was it celebrated before that? One might assume that at one time it was purely a Christian feast kept by the Christian Church and yet over the centuries it has clearly also become a secular celebration and never more obviously so than in our own day and age. Our Christian feast has effectively been hijacked – how can we rescue it? How can we put Christ back into Christmas before we lose our grasp on it completely?

The commercialisation of Christmas has almost completely overwhelmed even the remotest connection there might once have been with what the feast is actually all about, and the process seems to begin earlier every year. One well-known London department store takes great pride in being the first to put its Christmas wares on sale[7], a pride that has nothing to do with Christmas but with cornering the market before anyone else. Not to be too outdone, everyone else is soon climbing on board.

We then have the growing practice (imported from America) of decorating the exterior of houses and gardens in a vast and often extremely tacky illuminated effort to out-do the neighbours, an effort that switches on as early as November. What does this have to do with Christmas, the *real* Christmas, the celebration of the birth of Christ? Not a lot – in fact nothing at all. Just look at the decorations: Santa Clauses, reindeers, snowmen, holly, and all those lights – but is there a manger or anything religious anywhere to be seen? Usually not, and it's the same with town and city-centre Christmas lights.

And a walk through any card shop will leave you struggling to find a Christmas card design that's even remotely religious (they are more often found in the charity shops). It's all to do with political correctness of course – we aren't allowed to offend those who don't believe in Christ by reminding them that Christmas is actually a Christian celebration! But then why would anyone want to buy a Christmas card who doesn't believe in Christ and therefore what is the point of producing Christmas cards without a religious theme? I'm reminded of when I was working in Saudi. If you knew where to shop you could find "Christmas" cards but they all they said, very simply and blandly, was "Happy Holidays" and were purely secular in design. Under the circumstances, being in a conservative Muslim country, I could accept that, but not here.

Buying and sending religious-theme cards only is just the first of many steps we can take in the process of reclaiming the feast, putting Christ back into Christmas. Not only would we be supporting the manufacturers who have the courage to produce such cards but, more importantly, we would be bearing witness to our faith to those who receive cards from us. What we would be saying is: this is what Christmas is really all about and we are not going to apologise for it.

And, yes, of course we should celebrate Christmas in other than religious ways, but what aspects of society's "Christmas" are appropriate and which are not? The bottom line for us as Christians is that it's the celebration of the birth of Christ, and our priority should be the spiritual aspects of the feast and of the Christmas season, which, again, doesn't begin until December 25th and continues until the Epiphany. We are not being Scrooges, we are being witnesses to Christ – which is our call from our baptism.

So then, in what other ways can we try to put Christ back into Christmas? Food for thought and prayer.

*

As hopefully we try to defend our spiritual principles and priorities to the people and society around us, we also need to somehow communicate them to our children because ours is small voice among many much louder voices that convey often very different and quite contrary messages to them. It's a little like the Jewish "Family Seder" meal celebrated at Passover. The ritual allows for the youngest child in the family to keep asking: "Why is this night different? What is the meaning of what we are doing?" And, in answer, the accompanying scripture readings and lessons tell the story of Passover commemorated in the meal. It should be the same with ourselves and Christmas. Our children may not always ask the question directly but we have got to give the answer, teach the lesson, and ensure that the right message – the *Christian* message – is being conveyed and learned, otherwise there is a danger that it will be lost to them for ever. "Why is Christmas night different? What is the meaning of what we are doing?" What is our answer and what are we doing to defend, support and promote that reality for them?

## NOTES

1 And, again, especially when bought for children to use, they should be religious themed – usually a manger scene – the windows of which gradually reveal components of the Christmas story. Secular themed so-called "Advent" calendars revealing chocolates or the like behind each window do nothing to teach what Advent and Christmas are about; all they do is to teach children to look forward to more of the same in their Christmas presents.

2 "Yule" was the name given to the pagan winter solstice and meant "wheel" – the pagan symbol for the sun. Yule logs were burned in honour of the sun. Mistletoe was considered a sacred plant and kissing underneath mistletoe was a fertility ritual. Holly berries were thought to be a food of the gods.
[see www.the-north-pole.com/history]

3 The custom started in the Baltic countries and northern Germany. The first documented use of an evergreen tree at Christmas was in Latvia in 1510. [ditto]

4 The names of Santa's reindeer were first listed by the poem's author, Clement Clark Moore. Rudolph the red-nosed reindeer was an advertising creation of the American catalogue company Montgomery Ward as recently as 1939. [ditto]

5 *Steve Wright's Book of Factoids* (HarperCollins).

6 In a late 1800s issue of *Harper's* magazine, the illustrator Thomas Nast depicted the rotund Santa and added such details as Santa's workshop located at the North Pole and the idea of a list of good and bad children. [ditto]

7 Sometime in early summer if memory serves.

19

# VOCATIONS

> A few reflections by way of encouraging those whom God may be calling to priesthood or religious life to be open to that possibility. An encouragement, too, for prayer for vocations.

## God may be calling, but is anyone listening?

*But they will not ask his help unless they believe in him, and they will not believe in him unless they have heard of him, and they will not hear of him unless they get a preacher, and they will never have a preacher unless one is sent.*

(Romans 10)

Everyone expects that their parish will always have a priest to celebrate Mass and the sacraments, but how can that be if no one is supporting (actively and through prayer) the possibility of vocation to the priesthood? Because there are fewer priests in parishes than ever before, the potential for any influence that they may have with young people is basically limited to Mass times unless there happens to be a priest-chaplain in their school. Once upon a time many Catholic children, at some point in their education, came under the influence of nuns and, in some cases, brothers and were therefore quite familiar with them. These days, unless there is a parish sister, very few children ever come into contact with, or even see, sisters (or brothers) anymore, and how will it ever be otherwise if no one is encouraging (and praying for) vocations to religious life?

How can our young people be expected to consider the possibility of a vocation to a way of life they know little or nothing about these days? How is the voice of God, calling and inviting them, to be heard above the clamour of all the usual job and career considerations with which they are so much more familiar? Is consideration of a vocation to priesthood or religious life given due prominence by career counsellors in our Catholic schools? How comfortable would your son or daughter feel in bringing up the subject of a vocation with you? What would your reaction be? If it's something we don't really talk about, might this make priests and religious – and their chosen way of life – seem a little bit odd or strange?

In reality priests and religious are, by and large, quite normal down-to-earth people who simply listened to that small voice of God that kept working away at the back of their mind. All they did that was different was to dare to listen and let God show them what *he* (as opposed to everyone else) wanted them to do. He also gave them whatever grace and courage it took to make a different sort of choice for a different way of life than might ordinarily be considered the norm.

Of course such a way of life might not offer what the world considers "security" or "benefits", but that isn't what priesthood or religious life is all about. The spiritual benefits speak for themselves and as far as material security is concerned, through the generous support of the people God calls them to serve, priests have all the security they need – a roof over their head, money in their pocket (not a lot, but enough) and food on the table. They will never be out of work and when they retire their needs will be provided for – all of which gives substance to Our Lord's words in the gospel that a worker deserves his pay.

To find out more about particular religious orders, it would be better to contact them directly than for me to try to talk about them. Instead I would like to speak specifically about the priesthood.

At the heart of the vocation and ministry of a priest are the Mass and sacraments from which flow all the many other aspects of the spiritual and pastoral care that he may be called upon to provide. So, in addition to celebrating Mass and the sacraments, what else do priests do? Well, you name it: they serve in parishes; they are chaplains to schools, hospitals, prisons and ports; they work on the missions; they give retreats; they provide counselling and spiritual direction; they are preachers and teachers… the list goes on and on.

Priests also bring with them to their ministry whatever skills, abilities and experience they gained before they entered the priesthood. They don't emerge from the seminary like identical sausages from a machine; they are still who they always were with all that makes them an individual. Many had jobs and careers before they entered the seminary and, of course, they come from all sorts of backgrounds and walks of life. They bring all of this with them to priesthood and it hopefully makes their ministry all the richer.

At his ordination every priest is asked by the bishop: *Are you resolved to consecrate your life to God for the salvation of his people, and to unite yourself more closely every day to Christ the High Priest, who offered himself for us to the Father as a perfect sacrifice?* How this works out from day to day is a complete unknown until it happens. It can be a bit like a football match. Some days you just seem to wander round in the middle of the field and the ball never comes anywhere near you. Other days it's like being the goalkeeper with shot after shot coming your way requiring instant 100% effort every time – and no shot is ever the same.

When I first wrote this I made a list of all the things I could remember from a typical four week period in what was my parish at the time. In addition to the normal daily Mass schedule, there was the Chrism Mass at the cathedral and a golden jubilee celebration Mass. There were four funerals and therefore four visits to the families involved. There was the Easter Triduum to prepare for and to celebrate and Easter Gardens to set up in three churches of the parish. I prepared eight homilies. I attended four school governors' meetings. There were only two callers at the door but one was at 2.30 in the middle of a night when I really needed some sleep! I gave a talk to couples attending our marriage preparation course. I had a meeting with the diocesan accountant on a matter to do with taxes. I called in to the Easter Family Social and I spent one whole day waiting for deliveries to the house. There was also all the usual day-to-day, and weekly, administrative work to take care of. The assistant priest in the parish could probably give a very different list for the month but one nonetheless just as busy and typical of what a priest can expect to do. And important in all of this is the ability to be adaptable. You could be in the middle of a meal when a call comes to anoint someone who is dying or to pray with a family following a death. From there you head straight to school to talk to a classroom of children and then to a meeting with a couple who are planning to be married.

For someone giving even initial consideration to the question of a vocation, the prospect of giving up the things we are certain about to put ourselves totally in God's hands in this particular way can be very daunting. When society puts so much emphasis on a career and security, leaving everything to follow Christ can feel a bit like a high-wire act without a safety net. But then we need to remember St Peter walking on the water and that all was well as long as he kept his eyes on Our Lord and placed his trust in him.

After leaving school I started work as a lab technician, fully expecting that to be my career for the foreseeable future. Then along came my first experience of a call to priesthood (aided no doubt by my involvement in my parish) but, apparently, it wasn't to be at the time. Feeling I needed to be doing something active in the life of the Church, I ended up doing four years of lay-missionary work in Zambia and, as a result of my experience of the American Jesuits with whom I was working there, the feeling of a vocation arose once again and I spent two years in their Oregon novitiate until it became clear that, once again, the time didn't seem right. I then spent seven years working in sports and recreation in the Middle East and three years obtaining a degree in America, before my parish priest at home was instrumental in directing me back to the question of a vocation and off I went to Ushaw College and the rest, as they say, is history. It might be said that it took twenty years for me to find out what God was saying all along, except that I'm not sure the call was there all along. It came and went – or perhaps my listening came and went – until God was finally able to lead me where he seemingly always wanted me to be.

In trying to be sure of what God might be saying, it certainly helps to have another pair of ears doing some listening with you, listening to you, someone in whom you can confide and who will be sympathetic and supportive in the discernment you are going through. Most importantly, at some point in this process, you need to contact the diocese's

Vocations Director and seek advice from him. And, of course, essential to every step in this process is prayer – both your own prayer and the support of other people praying for you. The initial process doesn't require giving up anything you may currently be doing, it just means putting yourself in a position where you can listen more attentively and test what is going on.

God may indeed be calling – whether to priesthood or religious life – so dare to listen, dare to think about it, dare to pray about it, dare to find out.

In an address to priests during his 1982 visit to England, Pope John Paul said:

> *At some point in your lives, the call of the Lord to a special intimacy and union with him in his redemptive mission became so clear that you overcame your hesitations. You put aside your doubts and difficulties and committed yourselves to a life of total fidelity to the highest ideals of the gospel. Your free decision was sustained by grace. Lift up your hearts! Give thanks to the Lord for your wonderful vocation.*

And he later wrote, in a "World Day of Prayer for Vocations" message:

> *May the Holy Spirit make the entire Church a praying people who raise their voices to the Heavenly Father to implore holy vocations to the priesthood and to the consecrated life. Let us pray that those chosen and called by the Lord may be faithful and joyful witnesses of the Gospel to which they have consecrated their existence.*
>
> *Son of God, sent by the Father to the men and women of every time and of every part of the earth, we call upon you through Mary, your Mother and ours: may the Church not lack vocations, especially those dedicated in a special way to your Kingdom.*

20

# FAITH, HOPE AND LOVE

| |
|---|
| The title speaks for itself. |

*There are three things that last: faith, hope and love; and the greatest of these is love* (1 Cor 13:13). The theological virtues of faith, hope and charity (love) are, the catechism says, *the foundation of Christian moral activity… they are infused by God into the souls of the faithful to make them capable of acting as his children and of meriting eternal life* (para. 1823).

## Faith

We often use the words *belief* and *faith* interchangeably as if they mean the same thing. In some respects they can: my dictionary defines belief as *placing trust or confidence in a person or thing*, and faith as *a confident belief in the truth or trustworthiness of a person, idea or thing* – very similar. However with regard to faith, the dictionary offers a second definition which underscores the major difference between the two words when it says that faith is *belief that does not rest on logical proof or material evidence*. I *believe* that Australia exists, even though I have never been there, because I have seen pictures and I have met people who live there or have been there. On the other hand I have *faith* in the fact that Jesus Christ walked this earth even though there is no physical evidence, nor can it be proved by intellectual reasoning. I believe it to be true because God has said so. There may be various things that sustain my faith thereafter, but initially my faith is a leap in the dark – well, actually, a leap in the light.

The catechism offers the following thoughts: *To obey in faith is to submit freely to the word that has been heard, because its truth is guaranteed by God, who is Truth itself* (para. 144). *What moves us to believe is not the fact that revealed truths appear as true and intelligible in light of our natural reason; we believe because of the authority of God himself who reveals them* (para.

156). These statements presuppose belief in God, of course. If we don't believe in God, then we wouldn't have faith in the theological sense in which we use the word. For the sake of argument, and the pointlessness otherwise of going any further reading or writing this, let's say we do indeed believe in God – and, again, that involves *faith* rather than *belief.*

The author of the Letter to the Hebrews (11:2) and St Paul in his Letter to the Romans (8:24) say: *Only faith can guarantee the blessings that we hope for, or prove the existence of the realities that at present remain unseen... Our salvation is not in sight, we should not have to be hoping for it if it were.* The point being made is that whereas faith sustains hope in something as yet unseen, we need neither hope nor belief if the object is staring us in the face. Faith goes beyond belief in as much as, as we just said, belief can be sustained by proof and logical argument, whereas faith involves things that we can't see, physically or logically.

As the catechism reminds us, faith is a gift from God – a grace he freely gives in order to help us in the limitations of our humanness. Again this emphasises what we have just said, that we might believe something because we have worked it out for ourselves, proving it to our satisfaction, whereas the gift of faith helps us to accept things simply because God asks us to – whether they make sense to us or not. When we turn on a tap we believe water will come out because that's what usually happens – we have "faith" that it will happen because it always has done in the past. What God can sometimes ask of us is that we believe that water we can't see will come out of a tap we can't see. Through the gift of faith we trust not only that there is a tap, but that water will come out of it – because God has said so.

Sometimes people will get themselves in a state because they have found themselves questioning their faith. We probably need to understand the difference between "questioning" when it simply means working through things in our mind, and "questioning" when it means doubting or, worse still, refusing to believe. The former can be healthy as long as we are not putting our faith at risk – in a sense we are merely stretching our theological muscles, and that's fine if it doesn't lead to a need for proofs or persuasion. This is very different from what the catechism refers to as *disregarding or refusing to hold as true what God has revealed and what the Church proposes for belief* (para. 2088). We are in fact required, it says, *to nourish and protect our faith with prudence and vigilance, and to reject everything opposed to it.* "Lord I believe, help my unbelief."

## Hope

In the ordinary circumstances of our lives we typically hope for all sorts of things when there is no guarantee they will happen. Some of them will, because they fall within our own ability to bring them about; others are things that are probably more dreams than hopes. We may hope to take a foreign holiday this year; we may also hope to win the lottery.

Hope, in the theological sense, is a little different. *Hope is the theological virtue by which we desire the Kingdom of heaven and eternal life as our happiness, placing our trust in Christ's promises and relying on the help of the grace of the Holy Spirit* (para. 1817). *Through the merits of Jesus Christ and of his Passion, God keeps us in the hope that does not disappoint. Hope is the sure and steadfast anchor of the soul... a weapon that protects us in the struggle of salvation. We can therefore hope in the glory of heaven promised by God to those who love him and do his will* (para. 1820/21).

Through his death and resurrection we have been redeemed, Christ has "bought us back", we are offered the opportunity for salvation. However salvation isn't automatic. We can't say that because Our Lord has died on the cross for the forgiveness of sins that we can now "eat, drink and be merry" because it is all taken care of already. Nor can we say that because we believe in an all-loving Father, he will forgive us whatever we do. The catechism teaches that one of the sins against hope is *presuming upon God's almighty power or his mercy, hoping to obtain his forgiveness without conversion, and glory without merit* (para. 2092).

We are only too well aware that in and of ourselves we would struggle to merit the salvation offered to us – that's where grace comes in. *Moved by the Holy Spirit and by charity, we can merit for ourselves and for others the graces needed for our sanctification, for the increase of grace and charity, and for the attainment of eternal life* (para. 2010). By God's grace, anything is possible despite our personal faults and failings and limitations. No matter how much we may find ourselves struggling, there is always hope. No matter how many times we fall, hope helps us to our feet. There is always hope and hope offers encouragement.

*Christ has in fact been raised from the dead, the first-fruits of all who have fallen asleep. Death came through one man and in the same way the resurrection of the dead has come through one man. Just as all men die in Adam, so all men will be brought to life in Christ* (1 Cor 15:20-22). *I am the resurrection and the life. If anyone believes in me, even though he dies he will live, and whoever lives and believes in me will never die* (Jn 11:25-26). What greater hope could we have?

## Charity (Love)

*Charity*, the catechism says, *is the theological virtue by which we love God above all things for his own sake* (because he loves us) *and our neighbour as ourselves for the love of God* (para. 1822). Our love of God is lived out in and through our love and service of neighbour. *A man who does not love the brother that he can see cannot love God whom he has never seen* (1 Jn 4:20). A constant call in the gospels and letters of the New Testament is to love of God and love of neighbour – the "new and greatest commandment".

*The fruits of charity are joy, peace and mercy; charity demands beneficence* [charity or kindness] *and fraternal correction; it is benevolence* [goodwill or doing good]*; it fosters reciprocity and remains disinterested and generous; it is friendship and communion* (para. 1829). Unfortunately, these days, the word "charity" is used more with reference to donations and hand-outs to the less fortunate than in the theological sense of *caritas* – Christian love of neighbour. It is in this latter sense that we must understand it.

As followers of Christ, we are called to love our neighbour, even to love our enemies, but this isn't always easy. We may not always like certain people (indeed, they may make themselves un-likeable) but we do still have to love them – just as God may not always like us and the things we do and say, but he does still always love us. Perhaps, sometimes, the best we can do is to at least not wish someone harm, to at least be charitable (without being self-righteous about it) and in the meantime look for ways to move the situation in a more positive direction.

*This is my commandment, that you love one another as I have loved you* (Jn 15:12). Biblical commentators have suggested that when Jesus says to his disciples "follow me", he doesn't necessarily mean "follow where I go" but "follow my example", "do as I do". Insofar, therefore, as he extends his unconditional love to all people, this is the example we must follow. An essential input here would be St Paul's beautiful reflection on love in chapter thirteen of his First Letter to the Corinthians. Perhaps it would be good to stop and read that now. *If I am without love (charity), then I am nothing at all.*

The catechism goes on to make a further important point. *The practice of the moral life animated by charity gives to the Christian the spiritual freedom of the children of God. We no longer stand before God as a slave, in servile fear... but as a son or daughter responding to the love of him who first loved us* para. 1828). We don't "love" God out of fear, we love God because he loves us, and in his great love for us he gives us the supreme gift of freedom, freedom of choice, freedom to choose to love him. With that freedom God takes the very real risk that we may in fact choose *not* to love him, but what would our love be if it was coerced?

As we then search for ways in which to show our love for God, "the God we cannot see", one ever-present and practical way is through love and service of our neighbour, "whom we can see", in and through whom we find God. They are loved by God and in loving them we love him. And if we ever find ourselves struggling to find God in them, remember that they may be able to say the same about us, and in that there's a lesson about not being judgmental and the importance of reflecting faith, hope and love at all times and in all aspects of our life.

21

# GOD WILLING

> How much of an effort do we put into trying honestly and prayerfully to determine God's will for us? And what if our prayers are not answered in the way we hoped?

I don't know what you feel, but I have a slight problem with the gospel parable of the man invited to the wedding feast. The moral of the story is not to be presumptuous – that if we sit toward the top of the table, someone more important might have been invited and to make a space for them, we would be asked to move lower down. Instead, the story recommends that we sit toward the foot of the table in the first place so as to avoid such an embarrassing experience. But then if we deliberately sit at the foot of the table is it because we know our place, or is it because we hope the host will come and ask us to move higher and everyone will see it happen?

Something of the same conundrum can occur when it comes to trying to do God's will. How much of an effort do we put into trying honestly and prayerfully to determine God's will for us? Rather do we convince ourselves that what we want to do must surely also be what God's wants us to do? How do we know whether our choices are right, or whether we have merely convinced ourselves of the rightness of what we wanted to do all along? And if the outcome turns out not to be what we wanted, do we accept that perhaps we were wrong or is it easier to blame God for not listening to our prayers?

In his *Confessions,* St Augustine says: "All ask what they wish, but do not always hear the answer that they wish" and suggests that we should be not so much concerned to hear from God what we will as to will what we hear from him. Further food for thought comes from St Cyprian, commenting on the petition in the Lord's Prayer that God's will be done on earth as it is in heaven:

> Because the devil prevents us from obeying God completely in mind and in deed, we pray that we may will what God wills: humility in conduct, steadfastness in faith, modesty in speech, justice in actions, mercy in deeds, discipline in morals…to keep peace with our brothers and sisters, to love God with one's whole heart, preferring nothing to Christ… This is what it means to be a co-heir with Christ, to accomplish the command given by God, to fulfil the will of the Father.

When the rich young man approached Jesus and asked him what he must do to inherit the kingdom, he really didn't expect to hear anything in Our Lord's reply that he wasn't already doing. In his self-righteousness he was convinced that all was well between himself and God and Jesus would figuratively pat him on the head and say "Well done good and faithful servant – carry on". However he was in for a bit of a shock because things weren't in fact as they should have been and while his external actions and religious practices may well have been laudable, his wealth and possessions were getting in the way. That was the one thing the young man was trying to deny (at least to himself) but it was also the very thing that Jesus pointed to. If he really didn't want to know the answer, then he really shouldn't have asked the question. And this is how it is with us every time we seek God's will. Do we really want to know what his will is and are we prepared to accept and live with his answer? As convinced as we may be that God must surely agree with us, it may not necessarily be the case given that God knows what is best for us in a given situation. How, then, might we be more sure of God's will?

St Ignatius of Loyola was a great proponent of divining the will of God by what he called *discernment of spirits* – more of that in a moment. But his early attempts at discernment weren't always as theological as they might have been. Ignatius had developed a tremendous devotion to Our Lady and it is recorded in his biography that one day he was riding along on his mule when he caught up with a Muslim Moor and, in the course of their conversation, the Moor had said one or two things which Ignatius felt were offensive to Our Lady. So incensed was he that, from his still recent military background, he felt the only chivalrous things to do was to kill the Moor, but at the same time his newly re-acquired faith cautioned him against such an act. As they came to a fork in the road, Ignatius dropped the reigns of his mule so God could show him what he should do. If the mule followed the path taken by the Moor he would take it as a sign that he should go after him and kill him, but if the mule took the other path then the Moor's life would be saved and the latter is what happened!

Ignatius' later and more refined process of discerning God's will had its roots in his experience as a soldier, confined to bed whilst recovering from a severe wound to his leg. He had asked for something to read to help pass the time but all that was to hand was a book of romantic stories of chivalry and a book of the lives of Christ and the saints. While the former was in keeping with his courtly lifestyle, he found that the pleasure he gained from those stories was short-lived whereas when he read about Christ and the saints he found the inspiration they produced was much longer-lasting and, in due course, would be a major influence on the new and unexpected direction his life would take. It is that aspect of the results of our choices that is central to Ignatius' teaching on the discernment of spirits and which he refers to as *consolation* and *desolation.*

In his *Spiritual Exercises*, St Ignatius writes:

> I call it consolation when an interior movement is aroused in the soul, by which it is inflamed with love of its Creator and Lord... I call consolation every increase of faith, hope, and love, and all interior joy that invites and attracts to what is heavenly and to the salvation of one's soul by filling it with peace and quiet in its Creator and Lord. I call desolation what is entirely opposite of (that): darkness of soul, turmoil of spirit, inclination to what is low and earthly, restlessness rising from disturbances and temptations which lead to want of faith, hope and love.
>
> It is characteristic of God (when he) acts upon the soul, to give true happiness and spiritual joy, and

> to banish all the sadness and disturbances which are caused by the enemy. It is characteristic of the evil one to fight against such happiness and consolation by proposing fallacious reasonings, subtleties, and continual deceptions. It is a mark of the evil spirit to assume the appearance of an angel of light. He begins by suggesting thoughts that are suited to a devout soul, and ends by suggesting his own.
>
> We must carefully observe the whole course of our thoughts. If the beginning and middle and end are wholly good and directed to what is entirely right, it is a sign that they are from the good angel. But the course of thoughts suggested to us may terminate in something distracting, or less good than the soul had formerly proposed to do. It may end in what weakens the soul, or disquiets it…destroying the peace, tranquillity, and quiet which it had before (causing) disturbance to the soul. These things are a clear sign that the thoughts are proceeding from the evil spirit.[1]

When we seek God's will we must do so prayerfully and persistently, creating within ourselves a spirit conducive to listening peacefully for, and perceiving, God's response, detaching ourselves completely from any sort of predisposed expectation of what that response might be. Only in that way can we be truly open to all possibilities and therefore to that which is God's will. As and when we are sure of what we feel God is telling us, we should follow his lead and do what we feel he is calling us to do, but, as Ignatius cautions, we must test the spirits along the way. If what we feel we were led to do continues to produce a good feeling and peace of soul, then that would be a good sign. If, however, we begin to experience disquiet and a lack of peace within ourselves, then it is possible we may have made a mistake and our choice (or part of it) wasn't God's will after all. I say "part of it" because it's always possible that we set out on the right path, but were somehow led astray at some point in which case we have to go back in our minds to the point at which the disquiet and disturbance of soul began and try to discover what went wrong – if indeed we are sure things were right up to that point. It may be, however, that things were never quite as right as we thought and that our initial decision may have been more our own will than God's, in which case we need to begin the process again and hopefully this time discern his will correctly.

In seeking God's will through prayer of petition, we have to be open to the fact that our prayers may not always be answered in the way we hoped they would be. We might pray quite sincerely that God's will be done and yet, as we said earlier, we can be so convinced that our will and his must be the same that we just don't understand why our prayers appear not to have been answered – especially when they are about things like illness and suffering. In his lengthy pastoral *Letter to Proba*, St Augustine writes:

> If something happens contrary to our prayer, we should bear it patiently, give thanks in all circumstances, and have not the least doubt that it was more opportune for God's will to be done than our own. The Mediator gave us this kind of example. When he said, 'Father, if it be possible, let this chalice pass from me', he then changed the human will that was in him and immediately added, 'But not what I will, but what you will, Father.'

As Isaiah says, God's ways are not our ways, and his thoughts not our thoughts. Some things are beyond our understanding and remain, the theological sense, a 'mystery'. God always hears our prayers and those that are offered worthily will always be answered – perhaps not always in the way we hoped for, but in a way that God knows to be better for us – and not necessarily exactly when we expect (or demand!), but at a time that he knows to be more appropriate.

In his "No, Slow, Grow, Let's go" response to the experience of unanswered prayer, American pastor Bill Hybels writes:

> If the request is wrong, God will say, "No." Maybe the request is harmful in ways you don't understand. Maybe the request is self-serving, short-sighted, or even too small. God might have something better in mind,

and he's saying no to this one because he has a better plan. If the timing is wrong, God will say, "Slow". Like children, we dislike the words, "Not yet," as God shakes his head at us. God has reasons for his "Not yets"; we must not insist we know better than God. We tend to be much more concerned about comfort and convenience than about building character through patiently waiting on and trusting in God's timing. If you are wrong, God will say, "Grow". It's a lot easier to point the finger at God for not answering prayer than it is to look in the mirror and to say, "Maybe I'm the problem". Change your attitude on this or that. Stop that practice. End that pattern. Reconcile that relationship. Soften up in your spirit. Repent; receive forgiveness. When the timing is right, God will say, "Let's go!" and our prayer will be answered.

Knowing how important it is to seek and do God's will, the invitation at all times is then accept humbly and trustfully whatever his will turns out to be. In the seeking, the finding and the accepting, his grace is there to help us.

NOTES

1 *The Spiritual Exercises of St Ignatius,* Louis J Puhl SJ (Loyola University Press).

22

# FORMING OUR CONSCIENCE

> We are morally obliged to follow our conscience, but this begs the question as to whether we have fully and properly formed our conscience in the first place.

*Deep within his conscience man discovers a law which he has not laid upon himself but which he must obey... For man has in his heart a law inscribed by God. His dignity lies in observing this law, and by it he will be judged. His conscience is man's most secret core, and his sanctuary. There he is alone with God whose voice echoes in his depths.*[1]

## Following our conscience

*In all he says and does, man is obliged to follow faithfully what he knows to be just and right. It is by the judgement of his conscience that man perceives and recognises the prescriptions of the divine law.*[2]

*The voice of conscience, being the immediate perception of the divine will, is to be followed always, even when it is defective... It is right when its dictates correspond to the objective moral order... It is erroneous when it fails to do so.*[3]

The Church has always taught that we are required to follow our conscience, indeed – as St Thomas Aquinas has argued – it could be sinful not to do so if our conscience reflects what we believe to be God's will and therefore morally right. In other words, if we are convinced of the rightness of our conscience, then to choose to go against it would be to choose to do wrong and therefore sinful. For this reason we should never be forced to act against our conscience (which raises the whole question of, for example, conscientious objection to war). *Hence*, Lobo says, *the importance of forming a right conscience in which (our) judgement coincides with the objective will of God.*

## Forming our conscience

> *The more a correct conscience prevails, the more do persons and groups turn aside from blind choice and try to be guided by the objective standards of moral conduct... This cannot be said of the man who takes little trouble to find out what is true and good, or when conscience is by degrees almost blinded through the habit of committing sin.*[4]
>
> *Conscience must be informed and moral judgement enlightened. A well-formed conscience is upright and truthful. In the formation of conscience the Word of God is the light for our path.*[5]

Forming our conscience is a very different matter from persuading ourselves that what we have decided "feels right" and therefore must *be* right – and especially if it is what we wanted to do all along. The crucial point is this: is our decision what *we* want to do or what *God* wants us to do? How do we decide whether the two are the same?

Let's say, for example, that you are an avid walker and are planning to hike across an unfamiliar section of the moors. It would be at best foolhardy, and at worst potentially fatal, to simply set off in any old direction and walk wherever the whim took you. There could be all sorts of unknown hazards along the route you have chosen, and how do you know where you are going or where you will end up? It would be safer and far more sensible to plan your route meticulously, ensuring you have a current and accurate map – possibly even a reputable guidebook – and to have told someone where you are going and when you expect to be there. The question is: is it your choice to set off unprepared even though it would be totally irresponsible, or are you willing to take whatever time and research might be necessary in order to ensure a safe and enjoyable walk?

If someone steals something from a shop or, perhaps, from their place of work, they may justify their action by claiming that the loss to the shop or to their employer is negligible. What they have failed to do is to take into consideration the moral issue that they taking something that doesn't belong to them – in other words they are stealing. Justifying their action is very different from informing their conscience, which would involve taking into account the moral wrong and the sinfulness of their action and deciding (in conscience therefore) not to do it.

If we really want to know what is morally right, then we have to consider every possible source of guidance and information including scripture (God's law), Church teaching, and, if necessary, the advice of our priest or a spiritual director. If, on the other hand, we are reluctant to find out what the Church teaches and what is according to the will of God, then maybe that's a sign to us that we are more interested in the convenient and less challenging decision that we would prefer. Forming our conscience isn't simply about looking at options and then choosing the one that looks best or feels right to us – like looking in the fridge at all the healthy options and choosing half a cream sponge! We are standing before God and our decision-making process must therefore be honest and open – honest before him and open to his guidance and grace, otherwise he knows (and so do we) that we haven't therefore fully or rightly informed our conscience.

> *Return to your conscience, question it... Turn inward, brethren, and in everything you do, see God as your witness.*
>
> (St Augustine)

## Making up our own mind

> *The education of conscience is indispensable for human beings who are subjected to negative influences and tempted by sin to prefer their own judgment and to reject authoritative teachings.*[6]

Recently someone was bewailing the demise of most of our midweek holydays of obligation, now moved to the nearest Sundays. Basically this was done to protect the significance and sanctity of those days given that increasing numbers of people were simply ignoring them and therefore also ignoring the Church's teaching on the obligation to celebrate Mass on holy days. But then people are doing the same with Sundays as well, putting the celebration of Mass in second place to other activities that they decide on the day are more important. It doesn't seem to matter that a deliberate decision not to go to Mass on Sundays and holy days is a mortal sin – people are deciding for themselves what is sinful (even mortally sinful) and what isn't, what Church teachings they will observe and which they won't, even which of God's commandments they will keep and which they won't. We can't do this – we can't ignore God's law or Church precepts just because they may be inconvenient to our lifestyle, and we certainly can't decide for ourselves what is sinful and what isn't. Again we have to form (inform) our conscience on these matters and not just do what we decide we can justify, and God's law and Church teaching are central to that process.

Sadly this seems to be a reflection of what is going on in the society around us. People won't be told what to do and what not to do any more. It shows itself in a general lack of respect for those in positions of authority and for the law (or, at least, those aspects of the law that people find inconvenient) and those who have to enforce it. People are now doing the same with God, his Church and Church teaching.

In chapter eight of the first book of Samuel, the people ask Samuel for a king to rule over them 'like the other nations'. What they failed to remember was that they could never be like the other nations because God was their king, but they rejected his kingship for that of an earthly ruler. Repeating what we said right at the beginning:

> *Deep within his conscience man discovers a law which he has not laid upon himself but which he must obey... For man has in his heart a law inscribed by God... His conscience is man's most secret core, and his sanctuary. There he is alone with God whose voice echoes in his depths.*
>
> (Catechism of the Catholic Church, 1776)

NOTES

1 Second Vatican Council – *The Church in the Modern World*, para. 16.
2 *Catechism of the Catholic Church*, para. 1778.
3 *Guide to Christian Living (A New Compendium of Moral Theology)*, George Lobo.
4 Second Vatican Council – *The Church in the Modern World*, para. 16.
5 *Catechism of the Catholic Church*, paras. 1783 & 1785.
6 *Catechism of the Catholic Church*, paras. 1783 & 1785.

23

# "LATE HAVE I LOVED YOU"

Late-coming at Mass: a hobby horse of mine!

Speaking of his newly discovered faith in Jesus Christ, it was St Augustine who wrote: "Late have I loved you, O Beauty so ancient and so new; late have I loved you!" It would indeed be wonderful for someone to come to love of God late, but the same can't be said about coming to Mass.

Yes, I'm on my soapbox again but I make no apologies for it because what I'm talking about – our celebration of the Eucharist – is, as the catechism teaches 'the source and summit of the Christian life' (para. 1324). In its document *Celebrating the Mass*, the Bishops' Conference urges us "to deepen our understanding of why we celebrate Mass as we do (because) deepening our understanding of why we do something is often of great assistance to us as we seek to do things well' (para. 9). The bishops then go on to speak of the necessity for all of us to be open to ongoing liturgical catechesis because 'in these changing times it is not only children who need to be educated into a mature understanding of the liturgy" (para. 13).

A constant starting point for those of us who are "of a certain age" is the quite extraordinary practice – and it may never have been actual Church teaching – that as long as we were in church before the "*Sanctus*" we had "heard Mass", as we used to say, and in those days that could be at least half an hour into the Mass. It was indeed a bizarre concept that it didn't matter if we had missed the word of God addressed to us in scripture, as long as we were there for (what we today call) the Liturgy of the Eucharist and Communion, that was good enough. How could we have ever thought such minimal attendance at what was, and is, "the source and summit" of our faith life was acceptable, and acceptable to God?

As a further illustration of the approach to Mass back then, on All Souls' Day priests were permitted to celebrate three Masses on the apparent principle that if one Mass was good three must be better, and they would celebrate them one straight after the other! And the accepted practice was that if you came into church at a particular point in one of those Masses, you could stay to that same point in the Mass that followed and it counted as having heard one complete Mass! It was a bit like (again in the old days) missing part of the main feature at the cinema and sitting through the 'B' film and the "shorts" and watching the main film again until you came to the part where you came in. That might work with films but it should never have been acceptable when it came to the Mass.

Having said all of that, we knew – this time from Church teaching – that if we deliberately missed Mass on Sunday it was (and still is) a mortal sin and so if we arrived after that "cut-off point" in the Mass we hadn't "heard" Mass. If it was possible we would therefore have to come back for the next Mass. That's how it was, that was our understanding as to the legality of whether we had "heard" Mass or not and we were very clear on the subject. What happened, therefore, that it now seems not to matter whether we are late or not?

The Church teaches quite categorically that we can no longer see our celebration of Mass as just a matter of receiving Communion. The catechism says that the Mass *unfolds according to a fundamental structure which has been preserved throughout the centuries down to our own day. It displays two great parts that form a fundamental unity…the liturgy of the Word and the liturgy of the Eucharist (which) together form one single act of worship* (para. 1346). It would seem, therefore, that it may never have been officially acceptable after all to arrive in time for the consecration and still be able to say that we had heard Mass – we had missed one of the "two great parts that form a fundamental unity of worship".

I rather suspect (and this is only a personal reflection) that at a time when Mass was celebrated in a foreign language (Latin) by a priest with his back to the people, that it didn't seem to matter when we arrived or left because our participation in the Mass was so minimal anyway. The simple fact of our physically being there, and quite literally just "hearing" Mass was good enough. The Church now quite rightly stresses the importance of our full *participation* in the Mass, and that simply being there as a spectator is no longer acceptable because that's not what the Mass is about. *All have their own active parts to play in the celebration each in their own way* (para. 1348). It's a point reinforced by the Bishops' Conference when it says *the Church earnestly desires that all the faithful be led to that full, conscious, and active participation in liturgical celebrations called for by the very nature of the liturgy* (para. 24).

Crucial to full participation is our being there in the first place – and being there in time, not just for the start of Mass (as important as that is) but having the time to disengage from the outside world, place ourselves in the presence of Our Lord in the Blessed Sacrament, and prepare ourselves properly, spiritually, for the celebration in which we are about to take part. If we arrive too late to do that, then we haven't really given ourselves the opportunity to prepare as we should. Similarly if we have missed the penitential rite then we are not spiritually prepared for the celebration. If we have missed the priest's introduction to the theme of the celebration then we have missed information important to why we are there – and it *is* important. I find it very frustrating as a priest to spend that time (as the Church asks priests to) explaining, for example, the life of the saint whose memorial it may be, or briefly outlining the theme of the readings, not only to have someone arrive late having missed all of that but apparently feeling that it doesn't matter.

If we have missed any, or all, of the Liturgy of the Word, then we have not only missed God's word addressed to us, but we have also missed one of the "two great parts that form a fundamental unity of worship" and therefore we really haven't heard Mass (again as we used to say). The Church teaches that the Liturgy of the Word, as a part of that fundamental unity of worship, is no more or no less important than the Liturgy of the Eucharist. We can't content ourselves with arriving late for Mass on the grounds that at least we were there for Communion. "These two principal parts of the Mass are so closely connected as to form one single act of worship" (*The Celebration of Mass*, para. 20).

No one is trying to drive people away from Mass or say that they can't come in because they are late.[1] What is being said is that if we fully appreciate the centrality and importance of what it is we are celebrating at Mass then we should *want* to be there for the whole celebration, unavoidable one-off situations notwithstanding, of course. If we are late then we need to ask ourselves: was it completely unavoidable or is it happening quite often? Do I perhaps need to reorganise my schedule so as to make the sort of time I need for whatever other demands are going to be made on me before I head out to church or for the traffic I'm likely to encounter on the way? Do I need to take an earlier bus or could I ask a parishioner with a car to give me a lift to church? Is it actually quite possible for me to be at church in good time because of how important the entire celebration -from the opening Sign of the Cross to the Final Blessing – should be to me?

One further, and to me somewhat telling, point is the fact that we wouldn't be late for a film because we wouldn't want to miss any of the story; we wouldn't be late for a football match in case we missed a goal; we know it would be discourteous to be late for a play or a classical concert because getting to our seat would cause a disturbance; and being late for a dinner invitation would be considered bad manners.[2] Films or matches or concerts don't even begin to rate with the celebration of Mass – it's the single most important thing that we can do and will do in our day – and yet people will arrive late. Seemingly it doesn't matter if they have missed anything – even the word of God – and God isn't supposed to mind that they are late for his invitation. How do they rationalise these things?

Let's just turn the situation around – let's say that everyone was there for the start of Mass but were kept waiting, perhaps five maybe even ten minutes, before the priest processed out, and let's say this happened quite often – what would the people's reaction be? I don't think it would be very positive and quite rightly so. Why should they be kept waiting every week when Mass is scheduled to start at a specific time? And what does the priest have to do that is so important that he can't be there on time, properly prepared? Or let's say that the priest decided to skip the Liturgy of the Word and went straight to the tabernacle and distributed Holy Communion. Do you think the people would feel there was something missing and that they hadn't really been to Mass that day (which, of course, they wouldn't have been – not to Mass – in such circumstances)?

If we were invited to Buckingham Palace to meet the Queen, and all the more so if we were invited to dine with her, just imagine all the protocol that we would have to be aware of: how to dress, how to conduct ourselves, the things we can do and can't do, and how to address the Queen if she happened to speak to us. And, of course, we would be given a time to arrive by, after which we wouldn't be allowed in. If that is how things are in our approach to the Queen, how should things be in our practical and spiritual approach to God and his invitation to the Eucharist? The problem is that most of us would never expect to get an invitation to Buckingham Palace even once in our lifetime – which is why it would be such a major event if it ever happened – whereas we get an invitation to meet God in the Eucharist *every* day. Surely familiarity hasn't bred... well not contempt I'm sure, but is there perhaps a danger of taking the Mass, and even the Blessed Sacrament, for granted? Surely we don't need a reminder of God's almighty and glorious presence as recorded in Ezekiel[3] and Revelations[4] emanating from the tabernacle to get our attention? But when you see people come into church – God's house – and immediately start chatting with people, and they still haven't even acknowledged the real presence of Almighty God in the tabernacle and said a few words to him, you have to wonder. It's at *his* invitation that we are there in the first place and as Jesus teaches in the gospel (Mt 22:1-14) we should never take that invitation for granted.

The other side of the coin, of course, is that we shouldn't leave Mass early either. Mass ends with the final blessing and dismissal and nothing should be more important than receiving God's blessing and going in peace *when* the celebration – God's celebration – is ended. If we ducked out of a friend's dinner before dessert, what would that be saying and wouldn't it be considered bad manners?[5]

# NOTES

1 In the absence of a Catholic youth centre, as a teenager I used to attend a Presbyterian youth club along with my friends and, in an early and unofficial effort at ecumenism, used to occasionally attend their evening service (having already been to Mass, I hasten to add!). I always remember that their practice was to close (and possibly lock) the doors as soon as the service began and no one got in late (or left early) until the service was ended. It worked.

2 The Danish comedian Victor Borge used to include a routine in his American concerts, one that was set up beforehand but which he used in order to make a point. A person comes in late and is picking his way along a row of seats. Borge stops his act and asks the person, "Where have you come from that you are late? I've come all the way from Copenhagen and I was here on time!"

3 All of Ch 1.

4 Ch 1:12-18 and Ch 4:1-5.

5 Just before the end of Mass during the Pope's recent visit to Cyprus, an announcement was made telling people not to leave early but to remain in their places until the procession of celebrants out of church was completed. The doors were locked, it said, and no one would be allowed to leave early so please do not attempt to do so! This was no doubt done for security reasons, but it also indicates the poor practice that was presumably normal and was not going to be permitted on this particular occasion and shouldn't be happening anyway.

24

# BEING CLOTHED IN CHRIST AND FOR CHRIST

Some thoughts on our Christian vocation from the time we are clothed with Christ at baptism and a reflection on the appropriateness (or otherwise) of how we dress for church.

## Being Clothed In Christ

The word *prophet* can mean someone who predicts what is going to happen in the future. However, in the scriptural sense, it means someone who speaks up for God and the things of God.

In the First Book of the Kings there is the story about God sending Elijah to anoint Elisha as prophet. He is busy ploughing one day when, without any warning, Elijah appears on the scene and throws his mantle, his cloak, over Elisha, an action that he somehow seems to understand. We are familiar with the phrase "to take over the mantle" meaning to succeed someone in their position. Elisha's mission (if he accepts it) is, figuratively and literally, to take over the mantle of prophet. As Elijah is taken up to heaven, he leaves his cloak behind for Elisha, a symbol of his God-given authority.

During the sacrament of Baptism, immediately after the pouring of water, a white garment (usually a shawl) is placed over the baby and the accompanying prayer in part says: "You have become a new creation, and have clothed yourself in Christ. See in this white garment the outward sign of your Christian dignity." From that point onwards in our life we have been clothed in Christ, we have symbolically put on the mantle of Christ. Next comes the lighting of a baptismal candle: "This child of yours has been enlightened by Christ. He/she is to walk always as a child of the light." In both these actions we are given our Christian mission – to be witnesses to our faith, prophets for Christ responsible for the spreading of the gospel and of the kingdom.

It is precisely the same call as that received by the apostles – the word *apostle* simply meaning one who is sent. The apostles were sent out by Christ, taking up his mantle, "missioned" with spreading the gospel and witnessing to their faith, being prophets speaking up for God and the things of God: "Go out to the whole world; proclaim the Good News to all creation" (Mk 16:15). "Go, therefore, make disciples of all the nations… and teach them to observe all the commands I gave you" (Mt 28:19).

We are reminded of this same mission that we share with the apostles at the end of every Mass when we are instructed: "Go in peace, to love and serve the Lord". Go from this place, out into the world, and put into practice the word of God you have heard and live the Eucharist, the Communion, you have received. It's like running in a marathon and stopping briefly for a drink of water. We don't just drink for the refreshment that we feel there and then, we are re-hydrating our system for the miles we still have to run.

Being a prophet for Christ isn't always going to be easy. Remember the brothers James and John? Depending on which gospel account you read, either their mother approached Jesus or they approached him themselves, seemingly looking for some sort of assurance of the return they might expect for following him. Jesus says: "Can you drink the cup that I am going to drink?" (Mt 20; Mk 10). On another occasion he said: "If anyone wants to be a follower of mine, let him renounce himself and take up his cross and follow me" (Mt 16:24).

There will be times when, as followers of Christ, we will have to stand up and be counted. It can be a tough call especially when it means being a prophet – speaking up for God and the things of God – before family or friends. But we will never have to pay as high a price as Christ himself paid in his love for us. In our love for him are we willing to accept the (by comparison) insignificant price that witnessing to our faith and to what is right and wrong may cost us? "If anyone declares himself for me in the presence of men, I will declare myself for him in the presence of my Father in heaven" (Mt 10:32 – and let's hope we don't have to hear what he goes on to say in verse 33 about those who disown him).

Jesus also offered these words of encouragement: "Know that I am with you always; yes, to the end of time" (Mt 28:20). He is never going to ask or expect more of us than he knows we are capable of with the help of his grace – and that is always an important thing to remember… the help of his grace. If we think about St Peter walking on the water (Mt 14:28-33), doing the impossible with the help of God's grace, or of the well-known "Footprints" poem, God carrying us when life gets difficult, or dip into – and it's quite a dip! – the secular religion of football and the Anfield anthem "You'll never walk alone" (one of those references must be familiar), God is indeed always with us and so is his grace. It just needs us to remember it and to call on that help and strength at those times when we need the courage to stand up and be counted.

We have been clothed *in* Christ *by* Christ; let us then wear his mantle with conviction and pride.

## Being Clothed for Christ

During a recent visit to friends in America, they were telling me about a talk their priest had given at Mass on the subject of dress code. His point wasn't to lay down any actual rules or regulations on the subject, but simply to make the point that where people will dress formally for important social occasions or if they are to meet dignitaries, or that their places of work may require a particular dress code, they don't seem to consider that coming into God's presence in church warrants such signs of formality and respect. It's an interesting point.

People used to wear their "Sunday best" for church on Sundays and other important occasions – some still do – but by and large that seems to have gone as a practice. Of course it could be argued that God isn't interested in how we look on the outside and, certainly, coming to Mass shouldn't become a fashion parade. I think the point this priest was making had more to do with the basic question of whether we have really thought about what it is we are doing when we come to church, who we are going to meet (God), and whether the way we dress is as appropriate as it should be for coming into his house of prayer to celebrate the greatest sacramental event of our day or our week.

I don't know whether this is true in other nominally Catholic countries, but it is interesting that in Italy (and specifically in Rome) many churches enforce a very strict dress code. Outside of St Peter's for example, a church particularly popular with tourists, there are illustrated signs stating that men should be wearing long trousers and women shouldn't have bare shoulders or be wearing shorts or short skirts. Anyone not complying with this dress code is not admitted. This isn't the Church being prudish, but is a reminder to people that they are coming into a church and into the presence of God and that this requires an appreciation of the need not only for respect and reverence, but also for modesty – not always a widely held quality in our society.

By and large I think most people do dress appropriately in church – perhaps not necessarily in their "Sunday best" anymore, though at least that practice may have reflected people's awareness that where they were going, and what they were about to do, was special. Where appropriateness often goes out of the window, however, is at weddings and perhaps this is because there are typically a lot of people at weddings who are not ordinarily church-going. By the same token it is a sad reflection on our society that, whether church-going or not, many people seem to have no idea what it means to be in church and, in the case of a Catholic church, what it means to be in the presence of the Blessed Sacrament. Because everyone is probably heading directly to the reception as soon as the ceremony is over, they come to church in attire more appropriate for nightclubbing.

Aware of the potentially sexist minefield I may be entering into, in the case of men there isn't usually the same problem – a suit is a suit is a suit – but for women it can be an entirely different story. In the area of what might be politely called *décolletage*, between the bride, her bridesmaids and some of the assembled (female) guests, there is very often far too much *décoll* and not nearly enough *etage*! (as we might say). I've had one or two weddings where one good cough from the bride might have given me a coronary, and one, indeed, where the registrar (providentially seated nearby) had to come to the rescue of a bride who leaned forward a little too far to attend to the hem of her dress and, shall we say, lost control of the situation! Such styles and fashions, whether on brides or guests[1], are really not appropriate in church where we should be able to expect and experience modesty, reverence and respect.

It could be argued that what might be seen as undue conservatism could turn people away from church, but I would suggest, rather, that anything that promotes and preserves a sense of the sacred in our churches might well be more respected than giving in to the standards of the society around us. And, again, like that priest in America, I am not laying down rules or regulations, but just mentioning the subject as food for thought.

### NOTES

1 It certainly should be possible for female guests to wear a wrap of some sort, or a cardigan, whilst in church.

25

# RELICS

> Following the recent visit to this country of the relics of St Thérèse, some pastoral reflections for those who may have felt a bit guilty because they didn't share the euphoria that accompanied that visit.

Amidst all the euphoria that surrounded the visit to the UK in 2009 of the relics of St Thérèse of Lisieux, some may have found themselves struggling to understand what it was all about. Indeed the Archbishop of Westminster, Vincent Nichols, said in his homily: "This outpouring of faith has baffled many people. Some secular commentators have not been able to make sense of it all. I have found their incomprehension quite intriguing." It occurs to me that those who have indeed been baffled by what they have seen, may be feeling a little guilty about the negative feelings they have had, and so I thought it might be helpful to explore the Church's traditional approach to relics. (I should say at the outset that while I will try to be objective, I personally am not into relics as such – devotion to the saints yes, but relics no.)

The *Catechism of the Catholic Church* makes some important opening points:

> The religious sense of the Christian people has always found expression in various forms of piety surrounding the Church's sacramental life, such as the veneration of relics, visits to sanctuaries, pilgrimages, processions, the stations of the cross, the rosary, medals, etcetera (para. 1674).

> These expressions of piety extend the liturgical life of the Church, but do not replace it. They should accord with the sacred liturgy, be in some way derived from it and lead people to it, since in fact the liturgy by its very nature is far superior to any of them (para. 1675).

> Pastoral discernment is needed to sustain and support popular piety and, if necessary, to purify and correct the religious sense which underlies these devotions so that the faithful may advance in knowledge of the mystery of Christ (para. 1676).

Such devotions, and especially the veneration of relics, are in many respects fairly Catholic and so there is perhaps a danger that they may be misunderstood by others when they receive the sort of publicity and high profile that the relics of St Thérèse did. It is quite clear from comments made at the time that those for whom devotion to relics is not a part of their tradition, may well have struggled to understand what it was all about and, unfortunately, historical misunderstandings may have been rekindled. What has to be made clear is that we do not worship the saints or their relics. *The Concise Dictionary of the Catholic Church* says:

> The theological foundation for the cult of relics was developed in the Middle Ages. Stress was laid on the special dignity of the bodies of saints as temples of the Holy Spirit destined to a glorious resurrection, and on the sanction given by God in making them the occasion of miracles.

We are reminded that we share that same dignity, from our baptism our bodies too are temples of the Holy Spirit; we are all called to the sainthood of the redeemed; and the lives of the saints stand as examples to us that anything and everything is possible with the help of God's grace. They were ordinary people just like us, but who lived extraordinary lives. That's where the whole aspect of patron saints comes in and of having a personal patron to whom we can turn in prayer for assistance and encouragement as we strive, in whatever way we can, to follow their example.

The *A-Z of the Catholic Church* points out that "veneration of relics is not obligatory". I don't have a problem with relics *per se*, but I do have a problem with taking them on trips around the world as we saw with St Thérèse. My conviction is that if we have the degree of honour and respect that we should have for the saints, then we show that by leaving their bodies buried. I realise that it's a little different when we are talking about a saint, but how would we feel if someone dug up some bones of one of our family (and even took them on a trip)? I'm being a little facetious I know, because, as I say, we are talking here about saints and so the situation is a little different, but I think we would do better if we simply taught and promoted the lives of the saints and the spiritual qualities that have proved worthy of canonisation, holding up their lives (rather than their relics) to be emulated.

When I was parish priest at St Andrew's, Teesvlle, and the parish acquired its fourth church, St Anne's, I discovered a locked door in the back of the wooden altar. Eventually I came across a key that opened it. Inside there was a rather ornate box, about the size of a shoe box, tied with a red ribbon. It was filled with bones and there was some paperwork identifying them as the relics of St Eugenia about whom I knew nothing and about whom there seemed to be very little reliable information even on the internet. It really bothered me that they were there at all, but also, unlike the normal situation of a few small relics sealed inside an altar stone in the altar, these bones (and so many of them) were in a shoe box stored in the back of a movable altar in a church which was far from secure and which were therefore at risk if someone were to break in and do any damage. In consultation with the diocese, the plan was to take the bones back to Rome on my next visit there, but whoever the diocese contacted in the Vatican said they already had Eugenia(!). Whether this was a different Eugenia, or some other bones of the same Eugenia, there was no way of knowing. In the event, one of our local funeral directors agreed to manufacture a small casket into which the bones were placed and they are now in the burial plot at the Cathedral – buried as they should always have been ("earth to earth, ashes to ashes, dust to dust") rather than being stuck in a shoe box in the back of an altar.

Looking at what I have referred to as the euphoria surrounding the visit of St Thérèse's relics to this country, I couldn't help wondering how much of it was yet another example of our current fascination with "celebrity" – wanting to see famous people, even to touch them, or to be where they have been? Hopefully it was much more a case of people choosing to reverence the relics as a more tangible expression of their devotion to St Thérèse. The *A-Z* referenced above makes the same point:

> In accordance with the general human desire to treasure and honour relics of the great or famous (the bloodstained shirt of Lord Nelson, hair snipped from the head of a pop star), the Church has always encouraged the reverence to the bodies of the Saints which is represented by the keeping and honouring of relics. The practice is certainly as old as the second century. One of its earliest manifestations being the custom of offering Mass on or near the tomb of a martyr, a custom later incorporated into the Law requiring relics of a martyr to be sealed into an altar before its consecration.

This raises another question in my mind. If the requirement that there be relics sealed in an altar is purely to make a connection with the martyred saints of the Roman catacombs, that's one thing (as tenuous a link as it may be). Surely, however, the consecration of the bread and wine into the body and blood of Christ that takes place *on* the altar makes it infinitely more sacred than the presence of relics *in* the altar? And this connects with a further thought in light of the euphoria generated by St Thérèse's relics: why aren't there as many people packed inside the Cathedral and queuing up to get in every day (or at least on Sundays) given that Our Lord himself is really present in the Blessed Sacrament all the time? Is it a case of familiarity breeding not perhaps contempt (as the saying has it) but a degree of indifference? To put it simply: why don't as many people regularly pack the Cathedral for Mass as they did to see the relics of Thérèse?

What I would be afraid of is that, unless people's understanding is sound, there could be a danger of a degree of superstition creeping in. *The Concise Dictionary* (referenced earlier) points out that:

> In the West the cult of relics increased, especially during the Crusades, when quantities of relics, often spurious, were brought back from the Holy Land. They were kept in reliquaries, carried in procession, and often gave rise to superstitious practices.

Miracles were often attributed to the relics of the saints (though more correctly they would have been at the intercession of the saint him/herself – one of the items of evidence required by the Church in the process of canonisation) and consequently the importance that people gave to the relics themselves (and to touching them and so on) could, without care, verge on the superstitious. And the danger was even greater when there was money to be made from the visit of pilgrims to shrines and oratories containing relics (a common practice in medieval times). Our devotion should be to the saint whose relics they are and not to the relics *per se*. If we don't make that distinction, then the danger is that we might treat the relics as objects that could bring us good fortune, good health, etcetera, and that would be superstition. The relics are holy objects and that's why we honour and reverence them, but, ultimately, our devotion and our prayers should be to the saint whose help and intercession we seek.

I wouldn't want to deny for one moment the tremendous graces that were undoubtedly at work through the visits that were made to the relics of St Thérèse. As Archbishop Nichols said in his homily: "So many people find encouragement, perseverance and hope through the example and prayers of this most remarkable of young women." Perhaps the presence of her relics brought Thérèse just that bit closer to their lives. But she would surely be the first to make the point that people should ultimately be seeking not her, but Our Lord through their devotion to her.

And this takes us back to what we heard from the catechism earlier:

> These expressions of piety extend the liturgical life of the Church, but do not replace it. They should accord with the sacred liturgy, be in some way derived from it

> and lead people to it, since in fact the liturgy by its very nature is far superior to any of them (para. 1675).

All of the Church's sacramental celebrations and devotions find their source in the Eucharist. Nothing should become in any respect more important than the Eucharist, but sometimes devotional piety can come uncomfortably close to it. This point comes home to me on those occasions when people come into church and, without any reference to the Blessed Sacrament, go straight to Our Lady's altar, light a candle and pray to her, walk straight across in front of the tabernacle again without any acknowledgement of the Real Presence of Our Lord in the Blessed Sacrament, and light a candle at the Sacred Heart altar and pray there.

> Pastoral discernment is needed to sustain and support popular piety and, if necessary, to purify and correct the religious sense which underlies these devotions so that the faithful may advance in knowledge of the mystery of Christ (para. 1676).

It is to Our Lord alone that every saint (and Our Lady too, therefore) guides us through their intercession and the example of their lives. Our growth in Christ is the ultimate fruit of the honour and devotion that we show to them.

26

# SACRAMENTS: A CONSTANT SOURCE OF GRACE

A reflection on the help and strength and grace the sacraments provide at various stages throughout our lives, and the unique place of the Eucharist as "the source and summit" of our Christian life.

*A man is walking down the street one day when he falls into a hole. The sides are so steep that he can't get out. A doctor passes by and the man calls up to him, "Hey, can you help me out?" The doctor writes him a prescription, throws it into the hole and walks on. Next a priest comes by and the man shouts, "Hey, Father, I'm down in this hole, can you help me out?" The priest writes out a prayer, throws it into the hole and walks on. Then a friend walks by and the man shouts, "Hey, Jim, it's me, can you help me out?" Jim jumps into the hole. The man says, "Are you stupid? – now we're both down here!" His friend says, "Yes, but I've been down here before and I know the way out."* [1]

This is a great little parable that can be applied to any number of situations. In this case the man in the hole is us and God is the friend who jumps in with us. Through the Incarnation, God has shared our human condition, he knows what it's like to be human. He says, "I've been down there with you and I know the way out" – in fact he is the way out. "I am the Way, the Truth and the Life."

His first and constant aid to us is his grace, defined by the catechism as *the free and undeserved help that God gives us to respond to his call to become his children… infused by the Holy Spirit into our soul to heal it of sin and to sanctify it.*[2] It's a gift from God that is always there for us to call upon and yet all too often we try to deal with situations, occasions of sin, temptations or personal faults and failings all by ourselves and consequently it should be no surprise to us if we fail or fall. To use another little parable, it's like going for a bus and finding it already at the stop when we turn the corner. Do we simply not even bother because we know we've missed it, or do we break into a sprint, still miss it, but then – because we're so out-of-shape – have to sit down for ten minutes to recover? God's grace, in this example, would be checking on the time of the bus in the first place and making sure we were at the stop in plenty of time rather than putting our plans at risk – and our health!

God's other constant aid to us is the sacraments. The catechism says: *Christ now lives and acts in and with his Church through the sacraments… He manifests, makes present and communicates his work of salvation through them. They are the signs of grace, instituted by Christ and entrusted to the Church, by which divine life is dispensed to us.*[3]

The word sacrament comes from the Latin *sacrare*, meaning "to consecrate" or "to make holy". Just as we celebrate significant social milestones in our life's journey such as birthdays, marriages and anniversaries, one aspect of our sacramental celebrations is to make holy significant milestones in our faith journey too:

- When someone is born, in our culture we celebrate that birth, that gift of life, as also its yearly anniversary. In Baptism, we thank God for that gift and we welcome the person into the Christian family as they begin their journey of faith. Unfortunately we don't seem to do very well in celebrating our re-birthdays!

- As young people reach the "age of majority" and begin to take on new social responsibilities, this would seem another fitting occasion for a sacramental celebration. Whilst it wasn't intended as such, the Sacrament of Confirmation seems to have taken on that character, inviting from young people an adult commitment to their faith and the acceptance of new responsibilities within their faith community.

- The previously important social contract involved in marriage is being increasingly eclipsed by the choice of many couples simply to live together. However the Church continues not only to teach its moral message with regard to marriage, but also to spiritually celebrate and seal that vowed commitment, affirming its importance in and through the Sacrament of Matrimony.
- Socially speaking, Ordination to the priesthood celebrates a "career choice" though it is, of course, much more than that as a response to a religious vocation. As a sacrament it mirrors that of matrimony very closely, though it isn't always seen that way. A priest makes a vowed commitment not just to another person, but to the person of Christ and to all people as members of his body, the Church.

With each of these sacraments come the graces specific to them through the work of the Holy Spirit who thus provides the potential for our living out the particular stage in our spiritual life that we are entering into. Let's say, for example, that you have just been offered a job. The first thing your employer does is to make sure you know what you are expected to do and to provide the tools to enable you to do it. That's what the graces of a sacrament are all about – they enable us to accept and live out, spiritually and socially, the commitment we have made and the responsibilities that we have taken on. In that respect, to borrow a well known line from Gerry Marsden (and the Liverpool "Kop") we never walk alone.

Though slightly different in their purpose, two other sacraments also have parallels in our secular life:

- The Sacrament of Reconciliation (or Confession) involves not only forgiveness for sins, but also the opportunity for spiritual direction. It has been suggested that there might be fewer unnecessary visits made to counsellors of one sort or another if, where appropriate (and that is an important point of course), more people sought spiritual counselling from their priests.

- And when people are dealing with ill health or facing the possibility of admission to hospital, the Church offers the Sacrament of the Sick as a source of spiritual encouragement and strength and to complement and place before God the medical care they receive. When a person is nearing the end of their life then the Eucharist they receive as part of the sacrament becomes *viaticum*, "food for the journey", in preparation for their death which, as the final of our life events, will be marked by the social and spiritual ritual of a funeral.

In both cases the graces of the sacraments are very specifically healing graces – whether healing of the soul, or of the mind or body.

The remaining sacrament, the Eucharist (or Holy Communion), is described in the catechism as being the source and summit of our Christian life [4] occupying a unique place as the Sacrament of sacraments to which all the others are ordered [5]. It is the central and perhaps most important way in which Our Lord "makes present and communicates his work of salvation" because it is the gift of his very self, his body and blood, which he invites us to receive as spiritual nourishment and sustenance whenever we are able, and whenever we need, to do so. The symbolism of holy communion as a meal is particularly helpful in this regard. Just as we need to eat regularly to keep our bodies healthy and as a source of energy, so we can and should approach the Eucharist regularly as a primary aid to our spiritual health and well-being and to give us the sacramental energy (the grace) we need to live out our Christian vocation and bear witness to the gospel in our life.

I have used the following quotation from St Ephraim before. What he was saying was in reference to the word of God, but it applies equally to the sacraments and in particular those, like the Eucharist, that we can receive over and over again:

> *The thirsty man rejoices when he drinks and he is not downcast because he cannot empty the fountain. If your thirst is quenched and the fountain is not exhausted you*

*can drink from it again whenever you are thirsty. What you have received is your share, what remains is your heritage.*

If we were planning a long or strenuous walk, and especially in the heat, we would need to remember the importance of drinking plenty of liquids in order to keep our body properly hydrated. Everywhere these days, and not just on strenuous walks, you see people carrying bottles of water and drinking from them at regular intervals. This is how we might helpfully see the sacraments – again particularly the Eucharist – and the stream of God's grace that comes to us through them.

The thing is though, that we aren't always the best at asking for the help we need and that God offers. We put ourselves in situations of risk by repeatedly courting the occasions of sin that have caused us to fall in the past; spending time with people who can be occasions of sin for us, joining in the gossip, criticising and judging others, blaspheming and using bad language. At what point do we recognise what we are doing and do something else, something better, instead? At what point do we seek the help of God's grace to walk away, change the subject, or in some way speak up for God and the things of God? Whatever courage and resolve it may take, we won't be doing it alone if we seek God's help. All we have to do is ask.[6]

As we mentioned earlier, every sacrament brings graces specific to the occasion they celebrate. Those that we can celebrate over and over again – reconciliation, the Eucharist and the sacrament of the sick – are a constant source of sacramental help to call upon whenever we need it. To do otherwise is to set out on a walk but with no water, to sit by the fountain and not drink from it. If we fail not only to refresh, but also to "re-hydrate", our spiritual selves with the graces the Holy Spirit offers, then we run the risk of becoming increasingly parched and spiritually weary. To put it another way, they are a gift left on a shelf unopened.

As we strive for God's kingdom, we never do so alone. In the person of Jesus Christ, God has shared our human condition. He knows first-hand what it's like being us. If ever anyone was best placed to help us deal with life and deal with ourselves, it is God. His call to be holy as he is holy, to be worthy of the salvation he promises to those who are faithful, may sometimes feel like being in a steep-sided hole. God is the friend who jumps in, who enters into life with us. He knows the way out – he is the way out. His graces are there for the asking and his sacraments for the celebrating.

## NOTES

1 Overheard in an episode of US television series "The West Wing".
2 paras 1996 and 1999.
3 paras 1076 and 1131.
4 para 1349.
5 para 1212.
6 The old catechism used to talk about Actual Grace – "a passing grace (that we should pray for) which inclines our will to avoid evil and to do good".

27

# THE PRIESTHOOD OF THE BAPTISED

## (and the "Little Red Hen Syndrome")

We are constantly reminded that we are a "royal priesthood", but what does this mean in practical terms?

The Chrism Mass which is celebrated during Holy Week is basically a celebration of priesthood. It is the gathering of the priests with their bishop, in the presence of the people of the diocese, as a sign and affirmation of their unity of ministry in service of the people. The Oil of Catechumens and the Oil of the Sick are blessed, and the Oil of Chrism consecrated, by the bishop – oils that are used in various aspects of priestly ministry – and these are then taken back to the parishes as a link with that united diocesan celebration at which the bishop presides.

I dare say that the focus, prior to the Second Vatican Council, may well have been solely on the celebration of ordained priesthood. It was the Council that had the following to say about a concept which may have been new to most of us, that of the baptised priesthood of the people:

> The baptised, by regeneration and the anointing of the Holy Spirit, are consecrated to be a spiritual house and a holy priesthood, that through (Christian works) they may offer spiritual sacrifices and proclaim the perfection of him who has called them out of darkness into his marvellous light.

When we were anointed with the Oil of Chrism at baptism, the priest prayed:

> God the Father of our Lord Jesus Christ has freed you from sin, given you a new birth by water and the Holy Spirit, and welcomed you into his holy people.

> He now anoints you with the chrism of salvation. As Christ was anointed Priest, Prophet, and King, so may you live always as a member of his body, sharing everlasting life.

Just before that prayer I usually explain that chrism is a special oil used at baptisms, confirmations and the ordination of priests, and that it is also used by the Church of England at the coronation of kings and queens. It is this anointing which confers a share in Christ's ministry of priest, prophet and king – a ministry into which we are baptised and for which we are duly anointed or "chrismed" (Christ-ened, the name Christ meaning "anointed").

In one of the Easter Week texts in the Office of Readings[1], the writer says:

> Now that you have been baptised into Christ and have put on Christ, you have become conformed to the Son of God. For God destined us to be his children, so he has made us like to the glorious body of Christ. Hence, since you share in Christ, it is right to call you "Christs" or anointed ones… You have become "Christs" by receiving the sign of the Holy Spirit.

We are members of the body of Christ, we are priest, prophet and king because he is priest, prophet and king. We therefore share in the priesthood of all of the baptised, just as we also share the call to prophecy (bearing witness to God) and to a share in his kingdom and to rule with him in that kingdom.

At the Chrism Mass, following the priests' renewal of their commitment to their ministry, the bishop says to the people:

> Dear sisters and brothers, as God's holy people… each of us has a share in Our Lord's priesthood, given to us at our baptism and confirmation. So, in the name of the Church, I ask you if you are resolved to exercise that priesthood in the service of the Church?

Everyone present declares that they are and, presumably, if it had been physically possible to assemble the entire diocese for that celebration, everyone would have answered "We are". And yet, *are* we?

How do you picture priesthood? What do you expect of a priest? I suspect that most people's answers would have to do with ministry and service and, no doubt, the ministry part would have to do with those things that only a priest can do by virtue of his ordination. But if we accept that we share in the priesthood, in our case the priesthood of all the baptised, what areas of ministry and service are therefore open to us? And if they are open to us, are we carrying them out as enthusiastically and as readily as we should?

You must know the story of the *Little Red Hen*? Just in case you don't:

> One day the Little Red Hen found some grains of wheat and asked the duck, the cat and the dog if they would help her plant them, but they weren't interested, so she did it. When the resulting wheat was ripe she asked who would help her harvest it. No one would so she did it. She then needed help taking the wheat to the mill to be ground into flour, but once again no one was willing to help so she did it. Next she asked who would make and bake some bread with the flour, but no one would so she did it. When she asked if anyone would like some of the fresh baked bread to eat they all said yes, but she said no and ate it herself.

Parishes everywhere suffer from "Little Red Hen Syndrome". It's all to do with involvement or, rather, a lack of it. Let's take as a starting point the Catechism's definition of what a Parish is:

> A parish is a definite community of the Christian faithful. It is the place where (they) can be gathered together for the Sunday celebration of the Eucharist. It gathers them together in this celebration; it teaches Christ's saving doctrine; it practises the charity of the Lord in good works and brotherly love.[2]

The Second Vatican Council's *Decree on the Apostolate of Lay People* adds:

> Their action within the Church communities is so necessary that without it the apostolate of the pastors will frequently be unable to obtain its full effect... Nourished by their active participation in the liturgical life of their community, they engage zealously in its apostolic works... By their expert assistance they increase the efficacy of the care of souls as well as of the administration of the goods of the Church. The parish offers an outstanding example of community apostolate, for it gathers into a unity all the human diversities that are found there and inserts them into the universality of the Church. The laity should develop the habit of working in the parish in close union with their priests... (and) according to their abilities they ought to co-operate in all the apostolic and missionary enterprises of their ecclesial family. (para. 11)

They may sometimes only sound like "buzz words", but we really do have to think about our parish not just as a faith community, but as a faith family. We were baptised into the wider faith family of the Church at our baptism, but both spiritually and physically we are part of this smaller unit within the Church and the diocese that we call our parish. This is where many of you will have grown up; this is where you have your faith roots; this has been, and continues to be, your faith family – just as it is for everyone in the parish regardless of how long we have lived here. We are family because we were all (re)born into it through the sacrament of baptism. We are family because we are spiritually related – we are brothers and sisters of Christ. As every family *should* (in an ideal world), we gather together (daily if we can) to share a family meal – the Eucharist. Our parish church is our parish family home. And all of this has implications for us in terms of our involvement in, and the support we offer to this, our family.

The Church is everyone – *we* are church. The life of the Church depends on us and our involvement. It will be what we make of it and much of that will depend on the degree to which we accept our priesthood: our ministries and aspects of service. Again the bishops' question: *are you resolved to exercise that priesthood in the service of the Church?* What needs to be done? What could I be doing that I am not doing at the moment? What areas of service and ministry are crying out for my involvement? It's the old thing about "use it or lose it" – if I don't do it and no one else does either, then things will gradually grind to a halt because, quite simply, things are not getting done.

And I'm not talking about the things that more immediately come to mind, practical things like the sacristy and church cleaning and so on, as important as they are. I'm talking about the things that really challenge us in our recognition and acceptance of what the priesthood of the baptised is all about: ministry of the word, ministry of Holy Communion, pastoral ministry to the sick and housebound, music ministry, catechetical ministry, and so on. It's very easy to say we don't feel worthy to do some of those things, but then who is worthy? None of us is – in and of ourselves. We are worthy because God has anointed us at baptism and has called us to share in the life of his Son who is Priest, Prophet and King. You can't get anymore worthy than that.

## NOTES

1 The reading is taken from "instructions to the newly baptised at Jerusalem" but the writer is unknown.
2 *Catechism of the Catholic Church*, para. 2179.

28

# ENVY – AN 'OWNER'S MANUAL'

Looking at the subject of envy using quotations from various writers as well as my own thoughts on the subject.

*Envy is a symptom of lack of appreciation of our own uniqueness and self-worth. Each of us has something to give that no one else has.*

(Elizabeth O'Connor, spiritual writer)

It's a funny thing envy, well, not really, but you know what I mean. We don't really want it, we certainly don't need it, and yet so often there it is. Where does it come from and why, and what is it all about?

By definition it's a feeling of resentment brought on by contemplating someone else's possessions, qualities or achievements, typically with a strong wish that they were one's own. The word jealousy has almost the same meaning though it sounds slightly worse than envy in as much as it seems to have a nastier streak to it somehow. It's the negative aspect to envy that usually tends to bother us – and so it should – and that's probably why it comes up in confession as much as it does.

*Envy is the ulcer of the soul.*

(Socrates, Greek philosopher)

The catechism defines envy as "sadness at the sight of another's goods and the immoderate desire to acquire them for oneself, even unjustly". In this respect envy moves toward being sinful in that any such sadness could be a sin against charity, a resentment of someone's apparent well-being. It could even verge on breaking the commandment not to covet what belongs to another, and even, in the extreme, lead to stealing. We don't really know where the feeling comes from and we don't really like it because, left unchallenged, it can dominate us. Why should someone else's situation be such a problem to us? Why are we not content with our lot? Does it reflect a lack of gratitude to God for the blessings we have and which we perhaps don't appreciate as much as we should? – a thought we'll return to later.

I rather suspect that most of the time the seeds of envy are all in the mind. The things we find ourselves being envious about could well be figments of our imagination. We look at other people and we decide that they are infinitely happier, infinitely better off, than we are and we base this judgment purely on what we imagine to be the case, but often without any real evidence. How do we know how happy someone else actually is? How do we know how content they really are? We imagine that they must be simply because they appear to be, but we have no real idea what is actually going on in their lives. For all we know they may be putting on a façade of contentment and well-being in order to appear happy – and clearly it has worked, hence our envy.

But surely we have to ask ourselves, once again, why this becomes such a concern to us? – especially as it's none of our business. Why are we so fixated on someone else's apparent well-being? And why are we allowing it to so negatively affect us?

*Love looks through a telescope;*
*envy through a microscope.*
(Josh Billings, American humorist)

Perhaps we need to begin by asking an even more basic question: what sort of things tend to make us envious in the first place? Typically it is likely to be how together someone's life seems to be; how well-off they are; what a nice house they have; the places they go to on holiday; how perfect their family seems to be; how many friends they have and therefore what their social life is like; another's good health and mobility, even their younger age (especially if we are struggling); the talents and abilities someone has… and so on, and so on. Some of these things may be real, but they may just as easily be imagined – we don't really know, looking in from the outside as we are – either way, being envious doesn't do us any good, nor does it change anything. Why can't we simply be content with our lot instead of setting ourselves up for dissatisfaction by comparing ourselves unfavourably with others?

In a case of what we might call "para-envy", a reverse of envy, people sometimes also compare themselves *favourably* with others, a para-envy of how badly off others are. That's my theory as to why so many people watch, and are apparently entertained by, television dramas such as *Casualty* and *ER* and "soaps" such as *Eastenders.* If people can watch the (albeit fictional) suffering of others in Accident & Emergency units, or watch people screaming and shouting at one another in "soap opera" pubs and marriages and families coming apart at the seams, it makes them feel better about themselves and their own situation. It's a "there but for the grace of God go I" thing, rather than the "I want what they've got" aspect of normal envy.

> *Love is always patient and kind; it is never jealous and is not resentful.*
>
> (1 Cor 13:4-5)

On several occasions Jesus teaches in the gospels about the danger of being judgmental – and that is what we are doing when we find ourselves being envious of others. We are looking at them, or their situation, and we are making a value judgment, saying that what they have is better than what we have. Humility goes out of the window also because we are saying that we deserve to have what they have – otherwise why are we envious? And this can then lead us to be uncharitable because of the resentment the situation causes us to have toward that other person. Worse still, as we said earlier, it may also lead us into being covetous – desiring the things that someone else has – and here we are getting into the area of breaking commandments. In so many ways, therefore, envy is not a good place for us to be and so how can we help avoid it?

*Envy comes from people's ignorance of, or lack of belief in, their own gifts.*

(Jean Vanier, founder of the L'Arche communities)

Jesus spoke about stewardship of the talents that God has given us and how we will one day be asked for an account of that stewardship. We should be less concerned with what someone else has, what they can do, the opportunities offered to them and so on, than in how we are using the gifts and talents and opportunities entrusted to us. That's all that God is going to be concerned about. He won't want to hear how much better we might have done if only we had had the opportunities so-and-so had, or had we been as gifted as such-and-such a person. Rather it will be a matter of what we did with what was entrusted to us and how well (or otherwise) we used them in his service and to the glory of his name.

*Envy is the art of counting the other fellow's blessings instead of your own.*

(Harold Coffin, American humorist)

Do we sometimes fail to fully appreciate what God has given to us? It can be all too easy to fail in this area (not seeing the wood for the trees, as the saying goes) and a basic solution would be to reflect honestly and generously on just what we do have compared, certainly, to vast numbers of people throughout the world who don't have a roof over their heads, don't have adequate food or clean water, are suffering in poverty, and for whom death and disease is a way of life. Even here at home many people are a lot worse off than we are. An appreciation of, and gratitude for, God's providence to us will hopefully help to counter any envy on our part over what he may have given to others.

*To be rich in admiration and free from envy, to rejoice greatly in the good of others, to love with such generosity of heart that your love is still a dear possession in absence or unkindness – these are the gifts which money cannot buy.*

(Robert Louis Stevenson, poet)

Offering a particularly challenging thought, one of the prayers of intercession in Evening Prayer (Thursday, Week 3) of the Office ends: *help us to delight in the truth, and rejoice in your gifts to others.* If and when we look at other people and their situations, why is it easier to go down the road of envy than of rejoicing? We are fellow members of the body of Christ and our task is to build up his body, rejoicing in the "health" of its member: the gifts, the abilities, the freedoms, the strengths, the resources. It takes generosity of spirit – I was going to say *great* generosity, but it really ought to be our normal generosity. If we look at someone and see how well they are, how comfortably off they seem to be, or how free from concerns they are, then good for them, be glad for them. Being envious and resentful is self-destructive and serves only to detract from the health of Christ's body.

> *There is a variety of gifts but always the same Spirit working in all sorts of different ways in different people. The particular way in which the Spirit is given to each person is for a good purpose.*
>
> (1 Cor 12:4-7)

Having said what we have said about the negative aspects of envy, there is a more positive side to the word which the dictionary defines as: "a more moderate feeling aroused by admiration rather than resentment". We can say that we envy someone their talent or ability or the way they do something, but in that particular context we are paying them a compliment – there isn't really any actual envy on our part, nothing negative or resentful as such. If anything it is, as we were just saying, our rejoicing in their giftedness. In fact it's the sort of thing we would normally say out loud to others precisely because it is meant to be a compliment, as opposed to the negative feelings of envy that we usually keep to ourselves.

So there we are. We know where envy comes from and we know where it can lead, the question is: do we want to go there? Will envy control us, or will we control it?

29

# PRAYER

Some general thoughts and suggestions on prayer.

I am always a little reluctant to offer advice about prayer because, by definition, it's an expression of our personal relationship with God. Because most of us were brought up learning the formal prayers of the Church by heart, the legacy is that we are reluctant to move beyond that, as if it wouldn't be praying properly if we made up our own prayers. I fall into this trap myself every morning and night and in addition to praying the Office, always say the same five or six prayers of my own every day. In my defence I have to say that I say them because they are things I feel I should pray about at the start and end of the day, things not contained in as many words in the Office.

If we stop and think about it, prayer is simply conversation with God. If I met you in the street every morning and said the same five or six things to you every day you would think there was something wrong with me – even our compulsory conversations about the weather change from day to day! And yet I am aware that every morning I say the same things to God and can't help wondering if maybe he thinks there's something wrong with me. But I continue to do it partly because, yes, I would feel strange if I didn't say those prayers, but also because they are about things that I consider to be an important start to my day and if, over the years, I have evolved a formula that seems to best express what I want to say to God, then why change it just for the sake of change? (If it ain't broke… etc.)

At the same time, though, our formal prayers recited by heart can become very mechanical and we can experience a certain emptiness in our prayer life as a result. This is what I hear so often from people in confession when they mention concern over their prayers. Whether we pray silently in our heads (and hearts) or out loud if we are in a situation where we can do that, we know only too well that we can have finished our prayers and not remember a word that we have said. And it seems as if the more we try to concentrate the worse it gets because trying to concentrate itself becomes a distraction. Does any of this sound familiar to you?

I have this problem all the time with the "*Benedictus*" and the "*Magnifica*" in the Office – I say them every day, I know them by heart, and my mind just goes into "auto pilot" and can be miles away. Sadly it can be the same with the "Our Father" – a prayer that Jesus taught us but which, as a result, we say so many times every day that we don't even need to think about it – and yet we should. And then there's the Rosary; might it not be better to say just one decade meditatively than five decades mechanically?

The fact that we are praying at all is important. How *we* feel about our prayer is perhaps less important than how God feels about it and he would surely be happy that we are spending time in prayer. St Laurence Justinian said: "In everything we do God considers our disposition rather than our actions", and St Cyprian: "God listens, not to the voice, but to the heart." Perhaps it might help to use a candle or an icon or a water feature as a physical point of focus. Maybe we need to experiment with different types of prayer – even though we may feel a little guilty at first because we haven't said what we normally say. Try using your own words rather than formal prayer – talk to God in a natural way just as you would chat to a friend. In more meditative moments when circumstances are a little more conducive to this sort of time with God (away from distractions in a quiet room, turn off the phone and don't answer the door), try some spiritual reading or reading from scripture. And don't feel you have to read all of what you set out to read – stop and reflect on thoughts that strike you as you go along. Some quiet, meditative music in the background might help.

In any and all prayer we have got to learn to listen – an important part of prayer. Typically we are not comfortable with silence but how else are we going to be able to hear what God might be saying to us? As we noted earlier, prayer is conversation – dialogue not monologue – but all too often (and it goes back to how we were taught to pray as children) we do all the talking and no listening. And can we discipline ourselves to do absolutely nothing, for however long it takes, because this is time for God – for me with God?

*

In St Luke's Gospel (11:1-13), the disciples ask Jesus to teach them how to pray and so he teaches what we have come to know as the 'Lord's Prayer'. He then goes on to tell them a parable about the man who wakes his friend in the middle of the night to ask if he can borrow some bread so he can offer hospitality to another friend who has just arrived at his house. Jesus then goes on to teach: "Ask and it will be given to you…knock and the door will be opened to you" etc. The lesson of the gospel is that we should approach God in prayer with faith and trust, but also that we should be persistent in our prayers, almost pestering (though not quite nagging) God for what we want or, at least, what we think we want.

A little earlier in Luke's Gospel (18:1-8), Jesus tells the parable of the widow who keeps pestering an unjust judge until he finally gives in and listens to her petition – again a lesson in persistence. St Luke introduces the parable by saying: "Jesus told his disciples a parable about the need to pray continually and never lose heart". Our Lord was telling us to be prepared for the fact that sometimes our prayers won't be answered quite as quickly as we might hope. The *Jerome Biblical Commentary* suggests Jesus was saying that a delay offers us an opportunity to make ourselves a little more worthy of the answer we are hoping to receive, even, perhaps, ensuring we are as serious, as convinced, about our petition as we should be. St Augustine writes in his *Treatise on the first letter of St John*:

> Suppose you want to fill some sort of bag… You know how big the object that you want to put in and you see that the bag is narrow so you increase its capacity by stretching it. In the same way by delaying the fulfilment

> of desire God stretches it, by making us desire he expands the soul, and by this expansion he increases its capacity.

We are told to pray continually, a word which might also imply "consistently" – in other words that our prayer should be an expression of our on-going relationship with God. It is not at all unusual for people who ordinarily have no particularly relationship with God to turn to him when they are in trouble or in particular need. Suddenly they expect things of him, but the rest of the time what does *he* receive from *them*? – not that God's love is conditional, but you know what I mean. And I am certainly not suggesting that we need to bribe God into answering our prayers, but any areas for improvement that we might recognise should surely be improved anyway. If our prayer brings us to that point of realisation, then surely that can only be a good thing.

St Augustine in his long pastoral *Letter to Proba* offers some advice on the subject of our approach to prayer which I think may also be helpful to what I am saying. He writes:

> Why does the Lord advise us to pray, when he knows what is needful for us before we ask it of him? This can puzzle us, if we do not understand that our Lord and God does not want our wishes to be made known to himself, since he cannot be ignorant of them; but he wants our desire to be exercised in prayer, thus enabling us to grasp what he is preparing to give. We shall have the greater capacity to receive it, the more trustfully we believe, the more firmly we hope, the more ardently we desire.

He then goes on to look at the various sections of the "Lord's Prayer". It's interesting to reflect on how often we say this prayer – at least once a day for most people, perhaps far more often than that for others. Isn't that precisely an example of being persistent in prayer: not how often we say the prayer so much as how often we therefore make the same petitions to God that make up the prayer? And do we ever stop to reflect on how often and how faithfully he answers our petitions?

We can be quick to question why particular prayers seem to go unanswered and yet we can take for granted how many *are* answered and how many of our unspoken needs are provided for because God knows them even without our mentioning them.

This then brings up the whole issue of why our prayers are not always answered in the way we perhaps hoped. We might pray quite sincerely that God's will be done and yet be so convinced that our will and his must be the same that we just don't understand why our prayers appear not to have been answered – especially when they are about things such as illness and suffering. Back to St Augustine (to *Proba*) again:

> In afflictions that can both benefit and do harm, we do not know how to pray as we ought. But we owe this much trust to our Lord God, that if he does not take them away, we should not suppose ourselves to be neglected by him, but should rather hope with devout patience for good things greater than the evils.
>
> If something happens contrary to our prayer, we should bear it patiently, give thanks in all circumstances, and have not the least doubt that it was more opportune for God's will to be done than our own. The Mediator gave us this kind of example. When he said, "Father, if it be possible, let this chalice pass from me", he then changed the human will that was in him and immediately added, "But not what I will, but what you will." Hence, deservedly by the obedience of one man many are made righteous.

There is a call to humility in all of this: that, as Isaiah says (55:8-9), God's ways are not our ways, his thoughts not our thoughts. Sometimes some things are beyond us and simply lie within the realms of "mystery". God does always hear our prayers and those that are offered worthily will always be answered – perhaps not always in the way we hoped for, but in ways that God knows to be better, whether for ourselves or for others.

30

# HUMUS, HUMILIS

How do we understand humility and what does it mean to be grounded in our faith?

The word humility comes from the Latin *humilis* (humble), which in turn has its roots – no pun intended – in the word *humus* (the ground). Someone who is humble is therefore lowly, modest, meek – but not, we'd have to say, grovellingly so like that loathsome Dickens character Uriah Heep who was constantly reminding everyone that he was "ever so 'umble", a humility that was patently false, pretentious and manipulative.

The old "penny catechism" put humility at the top of the list of virtues, standing contrary to pride which topped the list of vices. Our current catechism speaks of humility as 'poverty of spirit': standing empty-handed before God, acknowledging our dependence on his providence, subjecting ourselves to his will and the guidance of his Spirit.

There's a story of a man clinging desperately to the roof of his house as the rain pours down and the flood waters are rising around him, and he prays to God to save him. A man comes by in a rowboat and offers to take him to a place of safety but he shouts back, "No thanks, it's OK, I've prayed to God and I know he'll help me". So the boat passes by and the rain keeps on pouring. Next a helicopter arrives and is preparing to lower a rope to him but he shouts back, "No thanks, it's OK, I've prayed to God and I know he'll help me". The helicopter flies off and the rain keeps pouring. Finally the house disappears underwater and the man drowns. Up in heaven he says to God: "I kept praying to you to save me; what happened?" God answers, first I sent you a guy in a rowboat and then I sent a helicopter. What more did you expect?" *Humus, humilis.*

Whenever we project our expectations onto God, or expect *him* to fit into *our* image and likeness rather than the other way round, it is essentially a sin of pride, a sin against humility. It's like Naaman, commander of the king's army, in chapter five of the first book of the Kings, who had contracted leprosy and was advised to visit the prophet Elisha who could cure him. But Naaman is so full of his own importance that he refuses to carry out the simple act of bathing seven times in the Jordan because he had expected some great ritual act of cleansing on Elisha's part so everyone would see that God had favoured him with healing. It's only when he shows some humility and does as the prophet asks that he is cured. So too with Jonah who originally tried to run away from the task God gave him to preach repentance to the people of Nineveh, but who then blamed God for wasting his time when the people did in fact repent and their destruction was averted. So also the scribes and Pharisees throughout the gospels who had their own faith agenda and resented Our Lord undermining their authority. Their answer was to get rid of the messenger rather than listen to the message. *Humus – humilis.*

We are called to a poverty of spirit which shows itself in an openness to God's action in our life – letting God be God. We need to reflect regularly on the story of St Peter being called out onto the water by Jesus, being asked to do something he knew to be impossible but learning, as a result, that with God all things are possible. He walked on water – or least for as long as he kept his eyes on Christ who had asked Peter to trust him and try.

When priests ask people to consider becoming, for example, ministers of the word or of Holy Communion, the answer is often "I'm not worthy". Of course they're not, and neither are priests to do what they do, but we keep our eyes fixed on Christ who calls us out onto the water and we trust him to make us worthy and able – otherwise why would he have invited us? Our response calls for humility, a poverty of spirit that admits that by ourselves we can't walk on water but we are willing to trust in God who calls us to try. Otherwise we are saying that God is wrong, and we can't do that. It also calls for a generosity of heart to use the gifts we have received in service of our faith community.

Someone may say: 'Ah, but it wasn't God who asked me to become a minister, it was the priest.' Well yes, but the invitation doesn't always have to come directly from God, especially if no one is listening when he calls. Then he gets someone else to do the inviting instead. I know this from personal experience.

I had been thinking about the priesthood on and off for years, but by 1987 I had possibly stopped listening to that "still small voice" and so God decided to step up the volume. My parish priest at the time asked me to come round for a cuppa, during the course of which he said he felt a vocation could come to someone through other people just as strongly and certainly as it might ordinarily come directly from God. He explained that a significant number of people in the parish, people who had known me since I first began experiencing the possibility of a vocation, had been asking him where I was these days in that process. As a result, he felt very strongly that I should once again give some serious thought and prayer to the possibility of the priesthood. A year later, I was accepted into the seminary and here we are.

We expect so much of God, but what can he expect – what does he expect – of us? There's an interesting lesson in the Old Testament book of the prophet Malachi (1:8). God sends the people, and specifically the priests, a warning through the prophet:

> When you bring blind animals for sacrifice, is that not wrong? When you bring the lame and the diseased, is that not wrong? Try offering them to your high commissioner, and see if he is pleased or receives you graciously.

It would seem that people were bringing defective animals to the temple for the priest to sacrifice, animals which were therefore cheap to buy or which they could afford to lose from their herds. (In today's terms, it would be like people off-loading their foreign currency, or a torn banknote, in the Sunday collection – which they do!) Presumably they thought God wouldn't notice, but more importantly it was symptomatic of their cutting corners, or not fully investing themselves, in their relationship with God.

Considering the root meaning of the word humility – *humus*, the ground – another sense in which I would use the word is in the need to be "grounded" in our faith, to have a knowledge and an awareness of the fundamentals of what we believe.

We now have at least two generations of Catholics who have been subjected to the political correctness of a national curriculum that required them to learn at least as much about other religions as they were allowed to learn about their own. With all due respect to other faiths, Catholic pupils attending Catholic schools should be learning about their own faith as a priority – that's what our Catholic schools are for. But if the Catholic faith is only one of many theologies being presented to them, it's no wonder pupils don't really know one from another. It's like being taught all about tennis and tiddlywinks and then being expected to play football!

I also have to say that I think the Church has paid a high price for allowing the old "penny catechism" to be phased out. That system of question and answer rote learning may not fit with today's educational methods, but it served the Church well for many generations. Those of us who used that catechism grew up knowing the basics of our faith – a solid foundation on which we could build throughout our life and one which we could refer back to as a source of what was right and wrong. Critics may say it was very legalistic, but that was the whole point: the catechism set out the basic rules and regulations, it grounded us in our faith. You can't send twenty-two football players onto the field and expect them to make up the rules as they go along – indeed, how would you know that twenty-two was a workable number of players in the first place? Similarly you wouldn't let someone get behind the wheel of a car without first having them learn the rules of the road and how to drive.

What we now have are two or three generations of Catholics who seem to have been taught little other than the fact that Jesus loves them, and his forgiving love then becomes an excuse for doing whatever they want, making up the rules (if at all) as they go along. God makes the rules, they are called the commandments, and the Church he founded supplements them with a few of its own – actually, therefore, his also. They are not optional. The consequence of doing our own thing is likely to be sinful but no one wants to be reminded about sin, especially mortal sin, and so they pretend it doesn't really exist. It does. We have a saying that where ignorance is bliss, 'tis folly to be wise, but that won't wash as an excuse with God with whom wisdom is bliss and ignorance is folly.

This is why there is so much emphasis these days on catechetics and adult formation in parishes because it is clear that there are a lot of holes in people's faith-knowledge that need to be filled. And yet it is typical of parishes everywhere that whenever courses or programmes are organised, only a handful of people come. Even for those who received a good Catholic education that process didn't end when they left school. We are never fully formed as Christians, we can't ever say we know it all or even that we know enough. Things change, we change, the world around us changes. And surely we're not too busy to come to courses and meetings occasionally? What other commitments could we possibly have that are so important that they take precedence? *Humus, humilis.*

We need to know our place before God. He isn't just another authority figure that we can challenge or ignore as happens with authority figures in society. He is our God; he is our life and our salvation; he is our rock and the foundation of our life. He is closer to us than we are to ourselves and so we can never run away or pretend he isn't there. In the person of his Son he has left us an example that we should follow in his steps (1 Peter 2:21). He washes our feet and then he asks us to wash others', to serve others. "He helps us in our troubles so we are then able to help others using the same help that we received" (2 Cor 1:3-4). *Humus, humilis.*

Being grounded in our faith is vital to our relationship with God. Humility, poverty of spirit, calls us to stand before God conscious that we are nothing without him. What he asks of us must take priority, all else is secondary. There are no days off in our following of Christ – but then why would we want days off? We were baptised for life not just for Sundays.

Why are our churches so empty? Why are our confessionals so unused? Why is Baptism the "Bermuda Triangle" of the sacraments, with people vanishing without trace immediately afterwards? What is the point of *first* Holy Communion when it is all too often also the last? What was the commitment of Confirmation all about if we are doing no more now than before?

Hopefully our faith hasn't become a burden that was loaded onto us by our parents and teachers and which we are now trying to unload and run away from like spiritual fly-tippers! It's who we are; it's what we became at our baptism. We can never be un-baptised. We can never "not know" Christ or the difference his presence makes in our life. In the words of John the Baptist: "He (Jesus) must grow greater, I must grow smaller." *Humus, humilis.*

31

## BEING A PART, NOT BEING APART

An appeal to active participation in our Eucharistic celebrations, a recurring theme throughout the Bishops' Conference document *Celebrating the Mass*.

I was recently reminded of an incident that happened many years ago involving a priest now deceased but who had better remain unnamed. About to begin Sunday morning Mass, he noticed a number of people standing at the back of church so he asked them to find a seat in the congregation with everyone else. Most did but one or two remained where they were, so he asked again saying that the Mass would not continue until everyone was seated. All but one found a seat. So he then left the altar and walked down to the back of church and told the remaining person that he could either find a seat or leave. He left and never came back again.

As a youngster I remember another incident in my home parish church. A number of people had come in after Mass had started and from the altar the priest actually asked them to leave and come back for a later Mass when they could be on time.

While we can't really argue against the principles behind both incidents (that wherever possible we should be in time for Mass and that we are meant to be a part of the single worshipping community and not keeping ourselves apart, unless we are unwell for example), understandably we wouldn't really agree with the way either priest handled those situations. By the same token, fifty years ago things were somewhat different and I think people would have been less shocked by either of those incidents than would be the case today.

In one of the video presentations that we have been using recently in the parish, it was interesting to hear parents talking about how difficult it can be to get a young family ready and out to Mass on time and also to try to arrive with some degree of peace of mind still intact after having to referee squabbles and arguments between siblings on the way. Those parents also spoke about how difficult it can be to focus on the celebration, or even to experience the graces it is meant to bring, when trying to keep young children under control and as quiet as possible can be so demanding and distracting.

And talking of distractions, something else I was thinking about had to do with people who find themselves easily distracted during Mass and their minds wandering all over the place other than being focused on what is happening at the altar. They do, of course, appreciate that the Mass is the single greatest miracle they have the privilege to witness and take part in and yet their minds are so often elsewhere. How can they stop that happening, they ask.

Let me repeat what I just said, that the Mass is the single greatest miracle we have the privilege to witness *and take part in* – and that's the important thing, that the Mass requires our active participation, and yet that is precisely what we so often struggle with for all sorts of reasons.

The Bishops' Conference document *Celebrating the Mass* says:

> Responsibility for the quality of Catholic liturgical life does not lie with priests alone. The fullness of all that the Eucharist can be implies the wholehearted engagement of everyone involved.

It goes on to talk about "active participation", "the participation of all", that parish priests should "promote the full and active participation of all the people", and says that everyone present at Mass "should contribute to the participation of all and show the Church as the body of Christ, actively engaged in worship of the living God".

At this point it would be understandable if you are wondering just *how* the people at Mass are supposed to actively participate. Isn't that the role of those directly involved in the celebration? Well yes, but it isn't just *their* role because in a very real way we are *all* directly involved. This can be a difficult concept to grasp and we have recent history to thank for that.

Forty-plus years ago it was accepted that all we had to do was go to Mass, just be there and do little more than join in the (Latin) responses. We used to talk about "hearing" Mass. We were merely spectators – we shouldn't have been, but more often than not that's all we were. It was like going to the pictures. You pay your money, you go in, you sit and watch for a couple of hours (you may even nod off for a while) and then you come out and go home. You might have slightly different expectations if you go to a play or a concert because at least you get to laugh and clap from time to time – which, if nothing else, gives you something to do and keeps you awake. If you go a football match you are, again, a spectator but there is much more opportunity for participation, emotional participation, shouting and cheering (or jeering) as the fortunes of your team ebb and flow. At least you feel like you've been involved – and at £500 or more for a season ticket, so you should!

We never should have been just spectators at Mass, an audience that never even got to clap or laugh or cheer. The Mass is a communal meal, a communal celebration, it's about all of us being there together, gathered around the altar just as the disciples were gathered around the table with Our Lord at the Last Supper. They didn't just sit there as passive spectators waiting for Jesus to feed them; it was a communal meal which they shared together, took part in together, served, poured, passed things and cleared things away.

Yes, the priest has a particular role at Mass just as Christ did at that meal and, yes, so do the servers and ministers who assist him and contribute to the celebration in a very direct and obvious way. But it's not just their celebration – they aren't actors on a stage for everyone else to sit and watch and listen to (though there is much watching and listening to be done). No, it is everyone's celebration, "the body of Christ, actively engaged in worship of the living God" as the Bishops said. But how do we participate, how can we be actively engaged, actively involved?

As I have just said, there is much watching and listening to do. If we went to a film or a play wearing a blindfold and ear-plugs, it would be a total waste of time. We go to listen, to watch and to be entertained. So too with the Mass and, yes, there is an element of being entertained at Mass but don't expect the priest to come out dressed as a clown and tell jokes. The "entertainment", the thing that should grab our attention and hold us spellbound, is the very fact that Jesus Christ our Lord and Saviour is going to become really and truly present on the altar in front of our very eyes under the appearance of bread and wine. If that doesn't impress then I don't know what will. Also in the Mass God himself speaks to us through his word in scripture. We'd be impressed if some celebrity was going to speak to us; in this case it's Almighty God through his prophets, through his apostles, through his Son. Jesus has "the message of eternal life" St Peter rightly said, are we impressed enough to be there on time to hear what he has to say to us? It's important and maybe, as that priest suggested, if we miss it we should come back to a later Mass when we can be there for the entire celebration.

Throughout the Mass we are physically involved through various actions and postures. Catholics are probably the most active of congregations because we stand, we sit, we kneel, depending on what is going on at the altar and we should think about why we are sitting or kneeling or standing: what is going on at that particular point in the Mass that makes that posture appropriate? We "cross" ourselves at the start and end of Mass, we sign our forehead, lips and heart at the Gospel, we exchange a sign of peace before Communion. Why? What do these actions mean? How do they relate to what is happening? Our actions shouldn't be just a matter of habit.[1]

There is also the whole aspect of taking in, and engaging with, the setting of the Mass – the liturgical colour, the decoration, the signs and symbols in the sanctuary, the music that accompanies it, all the things that are part of, and contribute to, that particular celebration. There is a real danger in taking things for granted, of not being observant, of assuming that everything is just the same as it was last week. The theme will be different[2]; the prayers of the Mass will be different; the readings will be different, the hymns will be different; and of course, *we* will be different. We come with different concerns, different needs, at the end of a week that has been different, and so what we bring to that celebration will be different and what we hope to gain from it will be different. In that respect the congregation will also be different even if most of the faces are the same.

Above all we meet around the altar as members of God's family. Just as you, as a parent, may have struggled to get your children up and out and to the church, so perhaps has God our Father struggled to get us up and out and to church (and on time). Just as you may find yourself struggling during Mass to keep your kids quiet and occupied and stop them fighting each other and distracting others, so God our Father may be having a tough time with us *his* children, asking us to be prayerfully quiet, trying to keep our attention, whispering in our ear when he knows we are being critical and judgemental of who and what we see around us, preparing us through word and action for the miracle he is about to perform for us on the altar.

Priests don't always get it right in their efforts to help the people to grow in their knowledge and experience of what the Mass is all about, but I hope we do at least try and we do have to persist in that effort because the Eucharist, as the catechism says, is the source and summit of our Christian life. It is too vital, too important, to our worshipping community and to the spiritual well-being of the body of Christ to settle for anything less. Indeed the *General Instruction of the Roman Missal* says:

> The Bishop should therefore be determined that the priests, the deacons, and the lay Christian faithful grasp ever more deeply the genuine meaning of the rites and liturgical texts, and thereby be led to an active and fruitful celebration of the Eucharist.

A final quote from that same document summarises what we have been saying (I have added the italics):

> The celebration of Mass, as *the action of Christ and the People of God...* is the centre of the whole Christian life for the Church both universal and local, as well as for each of the faithful individually. In it is found the high point both of the action by which God sanctifies the world in Christ and of the worship that the human

race offers to the Father, adoring him through Christ, the Son of God, in the Holy Spirit.

It is therefore of the greatest importance that the celebration of the Mass – that is, the Lord's Supper – be so arranged that the sacred ministers and the faithful *taking part in it*...may derive from it more abundantly those fruits for the sake of which Christ the Lord instituted the Eucharistic Sacrifice of his Body and Blood and entrusted it to the Church as a memorial of his Passion and Resurrection.

This will best be accomplished if, with due regard for the nature and the particular circumstances of each liturgical assembly, the entire celebration is planned in such a way that it leads to a *conscious, active and full participation of the faithful both in body and mind*, a participation burning with faith, hope and charity, *of the sort which is desired by the Church and demanded by the very nature of the celebration*, and to which the Christian people have a right and duty by reason of their Baptism.

NOTES

1 The speaker in the video presentation that I mentioned earlier gave two examples of this: of Catholics leaving their seat at the pictures and, out of habit, genuflecting to the screen(!), or of getting on a bus, "dipping" their hand in the used ticket bin and making the sign of the cross!

2 Which is why it is sad when the priest has introduced the theme and perhaps explained particular aspect of that day's celebration, and then people come rolling in late and have missed all of that and probably think it doesn't matter – and yet it does.

32

# FIT FOR THE RACE

How spiritually "fit" are we? How is our spiritual and sacramental life? How involved are we in the spiritual, pastoral and practical life of our parish?

St Paul writes to the Christians of Corinth:

> *All the fighters at the games go into strict training; they do this just to win a wreath that will wither away, but we do it for a wreath that will never wither.*
>
> (1 Cor 9:25)

In encouraging the Christian community in the practice and building up of their faith, Paul was using an example that would be familiar to them: that of the Greek athletes and fighters who would train long and hard in preparation for the competitions in which they were to take part and all for a simple laurel wreath awarded to the winner. (Would today's Olympic athletes settle for so simple a prize?) How much harder we need to train and how much more dedicated we need to be, Paul says, in order to strive for the prize that God holds out to us: that of eternal life. It begs the question as to whether we are as spiritually fit as we should be?

As a further example, are we as physically fit as we should be? I know I'm not. I used to be, but those days are long gone. When I was teaching and coaching sports in Zambia, I would play a full game of football with the students most afternoons, at altitude and in the African heat. I also coached (and played) volleyball, tennis, and badminton. I was fit, weighed ten-and-a-half stone but I was only in my early twenties. In my thirties I was in the heat of Saudi Arabia working in sports and recreation management, playing a little football and volleyball, and jogging and swimming for fitness. Even as a student at Ushaw I was still playing volleyball (and swimming) and giving lads half my age a run for their money, but once I was ordained and in a parish I became noticeably less active, less lean and less young!

But St Paul makes a good point. Those whose profession is sport or athletics have got to maintain a regular training regimen, a good diet and a healthy lifestyle. The pace and the physicality of modern sport demand no less. The rewards, of course, can make it all worthwhile for top-flight professional sportsmen and women, but they need to because it can be an all-too-brief career. While some may enjoy fame and fortune, others can be left with little more than the long-term consequences of repeated injuries and of pushing their bodies too hard for too long.

We all know regular exercise is good for us and many have both the time and opportunity to pursue it. Others, however, have the intention but it never actually translates into activity. It requires determination, discipline and getting into the habit, and it becomes all too easy to keep putting it off until tomorrow. We need the incentive, something to finally persuade us that the time is long overdue – stepping onto the scales, a visit to our doctor, a heart scare in a friend – something that finally gets our attention and makes us realise that our health is too precious (whether to ourselves or to our family) to sit idly by letting time take its toll.

Whatever we can say with regard to our physical health and well-being, surely the same is true, and more besides, with regard to our spiritual lives and, again, that was the point St Paul was making. We did RE in school the same as we did PE, but just as we never gave up physical exercise when we left school, no more should we have given up spiritual exercise. Trying to claim that we learned everything we ever needed to know about our faith when we were in school would be like trying to make the same claim about everything else in life which, of course, would be ridiculous. So how can we best ensure that we are as spiritually fit and active as we should be? What constitutes the *strict training* to which St Paul called the Christians of Corinth? Do we know what that involves but, like keeping physically in shape, lack the discipline, the determination and the habit? The incentive is our salvation.

- As we did as children, with our limited catechism knowledge, are we still going to Mass out of obligation and to avoid mortal sin? If so, that's a pretty sad reason for celebrating the Eucharist which should be, as the catechism says, the source and summit of our Christian lives. Could we get to Mass more frequently than we do at present?
- How regularly do we take advantage of the sacrament of reconciliation in order to ensure that our relationship with God and our neighbour is all that it should be?
- How is our prayer life? – not necessarily in terms of the quality of our prayer though that is important, but, perhaps, in terms of how much time we make for God in our day.
- Have we ever considered going on a retreat? If we have been on one, how long ago was it?
- When was the last time we spent time reading the word of God in scripture? Do we read spiritual writings as regularly as we read other books? – how else can we fresh and renew our spiritual knowledge and perspective. Have we read the *Catechism of the Catholic Church*?
- When was the last time we attended adult formation talks or presentations in the parish? If there was the opportunity but we decided against it, why was that?
- How involved are we in the practical, spiritual and liturgical life of our parish? If we aren't, why is that? Our faith commnity is where our spirituality is nourished or should be, and if that isn't our experience, then maybe our involvement might be a positive contribution both for the parish and for ourselves.

We can't make sudden and excessive demands of an untrained body. Someone who lives a fairly sedentary lifestyle suddenly having to sprint to catch a bus is likely to end up in an ambulance instead. An aching back for a week can be the price we pay for an overly ambitious afternoon in the garden. We go for a brisk walk in the country and end up in bed the next day not even able to walk round the house. The same is true of our spiritual condition. If our spiritual exercise is limited to Sunday Mass and sporadic prayer time, then we may not be as spiritually fit as we think we are, or as we should be. We may feel everything is OK, but we'll only find out for sure when something happens to test that fitness or when we one day stand before God to be judged on our fitness.

33

# THE REAL PRESENCE

> What do we believe about the Real Presence of Jesus in the Blessed Sacrament?

Living here in Whitby and being a fan of the television series *Heartbeat* (which, sadly, has now stopped beating), it is always interesting to walk past locations in town where scenes have been filmed and, therefore, where well-known actors have worked. I think we all find celebrity interesting – and I don't mean personal fame but just the extra interest that we find in visiting places that are famous or where famous people have been.

Maybe this is what motivates people to visit the Holy Land, though I can't honestly say I share their motivation. Having previously lived and worked in the Middle East for seven years, a visit there wouldn't have quite the same cultural novelty for me. But I also think potential visitors in these charged political days need to give very serious consideration to the very real risk of terrorist bombings and indiscriminate rocket attacks. Do we really need to put ourselves, not to mention tour guides and drivers, at such risk? However, people do still go there and in considerable numbers and presumably their motivation, as pilgrims, is to see the places mentioned in the gospels and that are associated with Jesus.

To begin with I think we would have to go there with a certain degree of scepticism in the sense that, in many cases, we can't be absolutely certain that particular sites are what they claim to be – they *might* be but we can't always know for certain. For example, at the time when Jesus was born no one had any idea of the significance of that event or of who the baby was going to become and therefore why would anyone have made any particular note of exactly where it happened? We know it was in Bethlehem, but how could anyone these days know anything more accurately than that? So, wherever we might be in the Holy Land, for someone to say this is the exact spot where Jesus stood or where such-and-such a thing happened, well, I think realistically we might have to take that with more than a pinch of salt unless, of course, there is some specific archaeological or historical evidence to back up the claim.

Even with that awareness in mind, people still go there because they want to see the places they have heard about and visit the locations (though perhaps not the exact spots) associated with Jesus. It's that same thing we just mentioned: the attraction of standing somewhere where someone famous has stood – though, because in this case it is Jesus we are talking about, there is a lot more involved than just celebrity and such visits are actually pilgrimages.

But surely this should give us pause to think. Why would we want to travel all the way to the Holy Land in order to see the places Jesus may have known (though they are now completely changed and modernised), even to walk where he may have walked (though the paths and streets are now paved over), when we can see *Jesus himself* at Mass? And I say "pause to think" because we probably do need to stop and ask ourselves whether that is indeed what we do believe – and we *should* believe it because Jesus has said that's how it is.

St Matthew records that at the Last Supper:

> Jesus took some bread, and when he had said the blessing he broke it and gave it to his disciples. 'Take it and eat,' he said 'this is my body.' Then he took a cup, and when he had returned thanks he gave it to them. 'Drink all of you from this,' he said 'for this is my blood, the blood of the covenant, which is to be poured out for many for the forgiveness of sins.'

Jesus didn't say the bread and wine *represented* his body and blood, but that they *were* (and *are*) his body and blood. He himself said this and so to claim that the bread and wine are less than his body and blood is to call his word into question. In one of the Easter Week texts in the Office of Readings, an unknown writer, setting down instructions for the newly baptised at Jerusalem wrote:

> Do not, then, regard the bread and wine as nothing but bread and wine, for they are the body and blood of Christ as the master himself has proclaimed. Though your senses suggest otherwise, let faith reassure you.

When the priest says the words that Jesus said at the Last Supper and does what Jesus did, as Catholics we believe that through the consecration of the Holy Spirit the bread and wine become the body and blood of Christ. They continue to look like bread and wine, but they become his body and blood through the mystery we call *transubstantiation*. There is no rational explanation (that's why we call it a mystery – in the theological sense) but we accept it in faith because Jesus asks us to.

At Communion, we *hold* Jesus, the real Jesus, really and truly in our hands, receiving him in the form of the host[1] and in his precious blood from the chalice. Similarly when priests, deacons and ministers take Communion to the sick and housebound, they are carrying Jesus with them. Therefore they should do so reverently, praying to Jesus who is with them and ensuring that the Sacrament is being carried appropriately. If they are driving it may be an additional reason for keeping to the speed limit and driving courteously – Jesus is their passenger!

Understandably the very fact that, in faith, we accept the greatness of the reality of Christ's real presence, may make us feel we can't possibly be worthy to hold him as surely as Mary held him, and yet we are and we can, precisely because he invites us to "Take and eat… (and) take and drink" and, for ministers, that they are called and commissioned to their ministry. All the more reason, therefore, to recollect every time what it is we are doing, who it is we are receiving, even if it overawes us (as it should – every time) and therefore that we ensure that we do so worthily in terms of preparation and reverence (every time).

It lends a tremendous gravity to our response "Amen" to the invitation to affirm this is "The Body of Christ" and "The Blood of Christ" we are about to receive. That single small word is a profound act of faith: that we truly do believe. "This is Jesus, the Lamb of God" – who then needs the Holy Land?[2] We don't really need to see where he once was when, at every Mass, we can see where he now *is* – yes, in heaven where we can't yet see him, but at the same time really and truly present in the Blessed Sacrament on our altar where we can.

## NOTES

1 And we are invited to receive the host in our hand – do we think we never sin with our tongue?

2 I am being a little facetious, of course, because such a visit might be of interest in the sense of putting Our Lord's earthly life into its geographical content. Also, as I have said, such a visit takes on a very different dimension as a pilgrimage.

34

## THE POWER OF THE PAUSE

> A reflection on the word of God in the Mass and in *lectio divina.*

The Latin phrase *lectio divina* literally means divine reading and refers to a particular way of reading and reflecting on scripture (in particular) which I would like to explain. As a basis for this, I'm going to use the session we spent on a passage from St Matthew's Gospel during a recent retreat. But a couple of other thoughts first…

St Isaac of Syria wrote:

> In everything you meet within the Scriptures, strive to find the purpose of the word, to penetrate into the depth of thought of the saints and to understand it more exactly. Those whose life is guided by Divine grace towards enlightenment, always feel as though some inner ray of light travels over the written lines and allows the mind to discern from the bare words what is said with great thought for the instruction of the soul.

This is also the purpose of pausing between our scripture readings at Mass. We haven't anywhere near the time (or at least people wouldn't generally be willing to spend the time) that it would take adequately to reflect on the word that we hear in the readings, but by at least pausing between them it gives us the chance to reflect on what we have heard, and for that word to sink in a little, before moving on. We are, of course, encouraged to return to the readings in our prayer later in the day.

When we pray with scripture using *lectio divina* as a method, what we do is initially to read the passage and then go back and work through it sentence by sentence, sometimes even word by word, depending on how the reading strikes us (or how the Spirit takes us), dwelling on certain words or phrases and reflecting on them and drawing thoughts from them for however long it takes. It may in fact be that we never get through the whole passage the second time around, but that's OK. The gospel passage from St Matthew below takes about a minute to read, but in our retreat session we spent a further hour-and-a-half reflecting, as a group, on the content of the reading. That's what *lectio divina* is all about.

What I'd like to do is, firstly, give you the gospel passage to read through and then, secondly, to try to set out the way in which our group reflected on it and the thoughts that resulted from that process. Obviously you can apply this method of prayer to any passage from scripture, long or short, and hopefully it will help you to discover new depths to the word of God and new insights and reflections.

> Jesus left Gennesaret and withdrew to the region of Tyre and Sidon. Then out came a Canaanite woman from that district and started shouting, "Sir, Son of David, take pity on me. My daughter is tormented by a devil." But he answered her not a word. And his disciples went and pleaded with him, "Give her what she wants," they said "because she is shouting after us." He said in reply, "I was sent only to the lost sheep of the House of Israel." But the woman had come up and was kneeling at his feet. "Lord," she said "help me." He replied, "It is not fair to take the children's food and throw it to the house-dogs." She retorted, "Ah yes, sir; but even the house-dogs can eat the scraps that fall from their master's table." Then Jesus answered her, "Woman, you have great faith. Let your wish be granted." And from that moment her daughter was well again.
>
> (Mt 15:21-28)

*Jesus left Gennesaret*
How did those he left behind feel? – unsure, abandoned, bereaved? or inspired, encouraged, glad (no longer threatened by the challenge of his presence)?

*and withdrew to the region of Tyre and Sidon.*
Why did he withdraw? Perhaps he was exhausted and needed to recharge his batteries spiritually and physically. (We need to allow Jesus to be human and to perhaps experience some of the same mental and physical limitations we do.) Perhaps he needed to preach the gospel elsewhere – crossing borders into Gentile areas. Do we need to answer the same challenge in bearing witness to the gospel in unfamiliar, even threatening, situations? Do we need to recharge our batteries in preparation? If so, how do we do that?

*Then out came a Canaanite woman…*
From where did she come out? – presumably from her house. Perhaps someone had told her that Jesus would be passing…her daughter needed healing and somehow she had confidence that he could help – perhaps she had heard of his miracle-working. How long had she been waiting? In tending to her daughter's needs, was she afraid she might have missed him? Would he help her/could he help her? – she was a pagan Gentile. Suddenly, through the window, she sees him pass by in the street. Of all the people passing by, how did she know it was Jesus? She drops everything and dashes outside, shouting after him to get his attention.

*Sir, Son of David,*
She had done her homework; she knew how to get his attention. She first addresses him as "Sir" – official and polite – then as "Son of David" – his Jewish title (from her as a Gentile).

*take pity on me*
She asks him to take pity on her but, therefore, on her daughter also. "Take pity" – she had nothing, she could offer nothing in exchange, she was from the "wrong postcode", and a woman, and yet courageous enough to speak to this Jewish man.

*My daughter is tormented by a devi*l
*a* devil, not *the* devil – is there a significance in that? We may not always be attacked or tempted by *the* devil, but how

many are our "demons"? And she is tormented – something that is there all the time, every waking moment, threatening her health perhaps even her life, demanding her mother's care and vigilance round the clock. How many carers are in such a situation and are in great need of the same help and relief for themselves that the woman sought from Jesus?

*But he answered her not a word.*
Why? This doesn't sit very comfortably with our image of Jesus but, again, perhaps we have to allow his humanity to come out. He was exhausted from the constant demands being placed on his time and on him personally. He needed some time to himself and now here was yet another demand being made. Perhaps he was at the end of his tether. Certainly we can sympathise with Jesus in a situation like this. How do we so often react? Or perhaps he was just taking a moment to be able to respond calmly and compassionately.

*His disciples went and pleaded with him*
Maybe they'd been walking ahead of him and suddenly realised he wasn't with them anymore. Looking back when they heard the shouts of the woman, they found she had stopped Jesus and now they had to go back to try to rescue him. They tell him to give her what she wants so they can get rid of the nuisance she was creating – they were flagging also.

*I was sent*
"Sent" as if it wasn't his choice. How do we handle "being sent"? How do we come to terms with, and accept, God's will to go and do things we'd rather not do, or that we'd rather leave to others? (Also a useful reflection for a priest who may find himself appointed to a parish he might not want to go to, leaving behind somewhere comfortable where he would prefer to stay)

*the lost sheep of the House of Israel*
What does Jesus mean by "lost sheep" – who were the "lost sheep" of his day? Who are they in our own day? – non-

Christians? non-Catholics? the lapsed? sinners? Do we ever say "Us"? Can we admit our need to be rescued, saved?

*Lord*
This time she uses his theological title... a possible sign of her faith in who he is.

*help me*
and, again, her daughter. To help her is to help her daughter and vice-versa. If Jesus helps you, does he help your family? If he helps your family does he help you?

*It is not fair to take the children's food and throw it to the house-dogs...*
We may find this sentence shocking – was Jesus actually calling the woman a house-dog? We would prefer to think not and we look for another interpretation. It is often suggested that he may have been testing her faith... what would this say about our concept of a God who would take delight in testing those he loves and who come to him in faith? Jesus is actually quoting a proverb (one with which we are unfamiliar) and there may be a little humour in the exchange between them – and he would admire the woman's ability to match riddle for riddle. In any case he uses the "softer" form of the word for dog: "little" or "pet".

She has also returned to using his polite title, 'Sir'. Is she annoyed by what he has said and has returned to being formally polite? Perhaps not, because it hasn't dented her intention or her faith.

*Woman, you have great faith*
Not because she "passed the test", but because she recognised who Jesus was, her persistence, and her trust that he would respond to her request. Instantly her daughter was cured.

Our retreat director had earlier told us the story of a young boy who used to pass a sculptor's workshop on his way to school. One day curiosity got the better of him and he decided to look inside and see what was going on. The sculptor was about to start work on a large, cold block of marble. The boy left. Several weeks later he was again passing by when he remembered his previous visit and once again stuck his head in to see what was going on. The sculptor was just finishing off the carving of a beautiful lion. The boy was amazed and had just one question for the sculptor: "How did you know the lion was inside the block of marble?"

Working through that *lectio divina* we could say that Jesus brought out of the situation the beautiful lion – he brought faith out of the woman and brought wholeness to her daughter. By the same token it might be said that the woman brought the beautiful lion out of Jesus by reawakening his compassion when he was exhausted and drained from his ministry.

We do ourselves a very real disservice when we switch off because we have heard a particular gospel passage so often before. We need to read or listen to it differently in order to get more from it no matter how familiar it may be. It's an encounter with the word of God. We need to employ "the power of the pause" which permits reflection. We have to read ourselves into the gospel passage, be there watching and listening, reflecting on what was said and done. Can I apply it to me and my situation?

Yes, it's a time-consuming process and takes far longer than a cursory read would take. But this is the word of God – could there be anything more worthy of our time? Could time be better spent? And it is also prayer – time spent with God. Could time be better spent? How many times have you met the risen Christ recently? How many times has he tried to speak to you? In prayer – and in particular in *lectio divina* – we can do both things at the same time: meeting Our Lord in the gospels and, through the enlightenment of the Holy Spirit, hearing what he is saying to us. It takes time and it requires listening – "the power of the pause".

35

# VATICAN-LITE

An invitation to think about our approach to Church teaching.

A news report on Pope Benedict's visit to the United States suggested that one of his objectives was to challenge what the reporter called the "Vatican-lite" approach to Catholicism on the part of many American Catholics, the suffix "lite" normally being associated with certain brands of beer that are light on calories or low in alcohol content. The inference was that Rome was concerned that American Catholics may not always be as faithful to Church teaching as they should be, and areas such as contraception and abortion were given as examples. What has brought about this situation, and is it unique only to the Church in America?

In his book *Faith of Our Fathers,* author Eamon Duffy[1] writes:

> Roman Catholics have always attributed a special value to their Church's past, for they believe that the saving truth of God is encountered not merely in the pages of the Bible, but in the proclamation, worship and shared experience of the Christian community – that complex expression of lived faith which we call tradition. Yet in the latter twentieth century the Catholic Church underwent a dramatic and, to many, disturbing transformation, which seemed to open up a deep gulf between modern believers and their past. The reforms initiated by the Second Vatican Council, which met from 1962 to 1965, profoundly changed the experience of Catholics at every level... It was an exhilarating time, filled with the sense of momentous and life-giving transformations, the bursting of constraints and the opening of new possibilities.

Those of us who are, as they say, "of a certain age" were brought up in a Church that was very authoritarian and there was very little, if any, room for "thinking outside the box" as they say today. We learned the basics of our faith in question and answer form from the old "penny catechism" – rote learning, but at least we knew where we stood. It began with questions on faith and the twelve articles of the Apostles' Creed (including grace and sin), moving on to hope, prayer, and charity – that was the first 170 questions. The next 78 dealt with the God's ten commandments and the Church's six. A huge amount of what we had to know as Catholics was contained in that section alone. The sacraments followed (that took us up to question 314) and then we moved on to a series of lists that we also learned by heart: three theological and four cardinal virtues; seven gifts and twelve fruits of the Holy Spirit; seven corporal and seven spiritual works of mercy; eight Beatitudes; seven capital sins and their contrary virtues; six sins against the Holy Spirit; nine ways in which we could cause or share in the guilt of another's sin; three eminent Good Works; three Evangelical Counsels, and "four things to be ever remembered"! – 332 questions so far. The final 38 were about the Christian rule of life and daily (spiritual) exercise.

Modern educationalists may not have anything too complimentary to say about that method of learning and yet few would deny that we grew up knowing a great deal more about the basics of our faith than children seem to these days, but, like a lot of other things, it doesn't seem to matter. In our multicultural, diversified, politically correct society, they will know as much, if not more, about other world religions than about their own, and no one seems to call them to task for such lack of knowledge or practice of the faith. We at least had that much-tested, rote learning foundation upon which to build as we grew older and the theory was that that's what we were meant to do so as to develop a much more mature knowledge of our faith than we had as kids. And the Church encouraged that process by publishing, in 1994, a 600-page updated version of the catechism – no longer questions and answers but a text to be read and digested. Fundamentally nothing has changed, but the very obvious physical difference between the two catechisms is a clear indication of the extent to which our faith knowledge, and how we live that out, should have changed as we grew up.

It is worth repeating that nothing of the basics of our faith has changed – everything that was to be found in the old catechism is to be found, albeit greatly expanded and developed, in the new one. How is it, then, that the phrase "Vatican-lite" can be applied to the faith-practice of many Catholics today? Why is it that so many are deciding for themselves which Church teachings they will follow and which they won't? Q103 in the old catechism: *How are the faithful on earth in communion with each other? A/: The faithful on earth are in communion with each other by professing the same faith, obeying the same authority, and assisting each other with their prayers and good works.* The new catechism says exactly the same thing though in a little more detail: *Mindful of Christ's words to his apostles: 'He who hears you, hears me', the faithful receive with docility the teachings and directives that their pastors give them in different forms* (para. 87). *The Roman Pontiff and the bishops are 'authentic teachers, that is, teachers endowed with the authority of Christ, who preach the faith to the people entrusted to them, the faith to be believed and put into practice'* (para. 2034).

As we know only too well, no organisation runs smoothly without some degree of control and management, without guidance and oversight, policies and practices, and without the need for sanctions in the event that they have to be applied. Whether we like it or not, there will always be rules and laws; human nature being what it is we don't seem to be able to function without them. Football is always a good example. The established laws of the game, enforced by national and international bodies, ensure that it will be played in a specific and identifiable way anywhere in the world. A referee is appointed to apply those laws and everyone expects a match to be played according to them. Players can't suddenly decide for themselves that they are going to ignore particular laws simply because they don't like them. If they did, or if the referee failed to do his job properly, matches would descend into chaos. Another example would be the rules of the road. Imagine if anyone of any age was allowed to drive, with or without a licence, or if people could decide for themselves what speed to drive at and which side of road to drive on! And perhaps the most telling example of all, again from Eamon Duffy: "You cannot have soldiers debating the wisdom of their orders in the face of the enemy."

Even God found laws were necessary, or rather that the people of Israel made them necessary, and so he gave them (and us) his ten commandments as a minimum set of guidelines for living out their (and our) faith relationship with him. The Church has done the same thing through its precepts or commandments. We can't start deciding for ourselves which laws we will keep and which we won't, or which Church teachings we will abide by, first of all because we don't have that authority, but, secondly, because that sort of self-determination threatens the universal identity of the Church and the unity of the body of Christ. Being a follower of Christ isn't a buffet, a smorgasbord, from which we can pick and choose. When we sign up at our baptism, it's for the whole thing.

Duffy writes: "God calls us not into some future invisible Church, but to the responsibilities of a real community, which will support and nourish us, but which will also make demands on us, demands which may not always seem reasonable or right." The word *seem* is important in that sentence if we truly believe in the Holy Spirit guiding the Church and the God-given charism of infallibility in matters of faith and morals that she thereby enjoys. We should accept and follow because we are asked to and not because we are told to or have to. Fidelity freely chosen is a more mature response than obedience for its own sake. As a society we have laws and rules (many based on *natural law*[2]) designed to safeguard the social structures and values that are important to us and we punish those accordingly who disregard or break those laws. In an ideal world we shouldn't need such sanctions if everyone appreciated and accepted the mutual benefit to be gained from respect for the law and, more importantly, respect for one another.

"To reunite all his children, scattered and led astray by sin, the Father willed to call the whole of humanity together into his Son's Church. The Church is the place where humanity must rediscover its unity and salvation."[3] It is dangerously short-sighted to see the Church simply as an institution rather than the means to salvation which was Our Lord's intention in founding it. It reduces the Church to something "worldly" rather than "other worldly". People begin to treat the Church and its God-given teaching authority the same way they treat authority in general. Also, just as many people these days have no qualms about disregarding inconvenient aspects of the law – especially if there is little perceived risk of sanctions – such is their approach to God's law and the laws of the Church. As I've just mentioned, what is lacking is respect... that and discipline.

It doesn't really matter, as such, whether we like a particular Church teaching or not, or whether it is convenient to us or not. The Church isn't about us as individuals; it's about communion, about unity, about members of the body of Christ together. Again from the catechism: 'The comparison of the Church with the body (of Christ) casts light on the intimate bond between Christ and his Church. Not only is she gathered *around* him, she is united *in* him, in his body (and specifically in) the unity of all her members with each other as a result of their union with Christ' (para. 789). Whilst there are always going to be cultural differences within so universal a Church, we are called to a unity of belief which also means, with only minor (cultural) variations, a unity of practice.

As we learned from our 'penny catechism', one of the most severe penalties that could be imposed by the Church was, and still is, *excommunication*, but, of course, such a severe penalty is, in the strictest sense, imposed only by the Church in the most serious of situations. But it is worth thinking about the fact that if we choose to ignore, or even to reject, certain aspects of Church teaching, then in effect we are "ex-communicating" ourselves – literally separating ourselves, to whatever degree, from the body of the Church and in some cases we may even be excluding ourselves from receiving Holy Communion because the actions resulting from our choices may be seriously sinful. This was, for example, the reminder that Scotland's Cardinal O'Brien issued last year to Catholic

MPs who would have gone against the Church's moral teaching by a pro-abortion vote in Parliament. Their defence that they would have been voting for the issue at hand "in conscience" doesn't really hold water because, whilst we are obliged to follow our conscience, our conscience may be ill-informed. It isn't simply a matter of making up our mind and it certainly isn't a matter of coming to a convenient decision or one *we* are convinced is right. Deciding something in conscience means prayerfully considering all the information we can (from God's teaching and the Church's teaching) so that our conscience is fully and properly informed through and with the guidance of the Holy Spirit.

The call to unity and fidelity is a constant theme in the New Testament. "I am the vine, you are the branches. Whoever remains in me, with me in him, bears fruit in plenty; for cut off from me you can do nothing' (Jn 15:5). "No household divided against itself can stand" (Mt 12:25). "Holy Father, keep those you have given me true to your name, so that they may be one like us" (Jn 17:11). "If our life in Christ means anything to you, if love can persuade at all, or the Spirit that we have in common… then be united in your convictions and united in your love, with a common purpose and a common mind" (Phil 2:1-2). "Obey your leaders and do as they tell you, because they must give an account of the way they look after your souls' (Heb 13:17).

Selective observance, selective practise, in other words being "Vatican-lite", isn't an option – we don't have the authority. The real authority is Jesus Christ's, a teaching authority that he delegated to the Church he founded to be the means of our salvation. Through baptism we have been called to be members of his body the Church and to build up that body in unity and love, not fragment it through dissent and personal preference. The life of the body is the Holy Spirit: "If you love me you will keep my commandments. I shall ask the Father and he will give you another Advocate to be with you for ever, that Spirit of truth whom the world can never receive… he is with you, he is in you" (Jn 14:15-16). Only in unity in his body can we hope to share his Spirit and his life – now and for eternal life.

## NOTES

1 Professor of the History of Christianity, University of Cambridge.
2 A law of morality that derives from an instinctive sense of right and wrong.
3 *Catechism of the Catholic Church*, para. 845.